JUST GO
SAYA SAKAKIBARA

TURNING FEAR INTO
A SUPERPOWER

JUST GO
SAYA SAKAKIBARA

SIMON & SCHUSTER

New York · Amsterdam/Antwerp · London · Toronto · Sydney/Melbourne · New Delhi

JUST GO: TURNING FEAR INTO A SUPERPOWER
First published in Australia in 2025 by
Simon & Schuster (Australia) Pty Limited
Level 4, 32 York St, Sydney NSW 2000

10 9 8 7 6 5 4 3 2 1

New York Amsterdam/Antwerp London Toronto Sydney/Melbourne New Delhi
Visit our website at www.simonandschuster.com.au

For more than 100 years, Simon & Schuster has championed authors and the stories they create. By respecting the copyright of an author's intellectual property, you enable Simon & Schuster and the author to continue publishing exceptional books for years to come. We thank you for supporting the author's copyright by purchasing an authorised edition of this book.

No amount of this book may be reproduced or stored in any format, nor may it be uploaded to any website, database, language-learning model, or other repository, retrieval, or artificial intelligence system without express permission. All rights reserved. Inquiries may be directed to Simon & Schuster, 1230 Avenue of the Americas, New York, NY 10020 or permissions@simonandschuster.com.

© Saya Sakakibara 2025

All rights reserved. No part of this publication may be reproduced, stored in a retrieval system, or transmitted in any form or by any means, electronic, mechanical, photocopying, recording or otherwise, without prior permission of the publisher.

 A catalogue record for this book is available from the National Library of Australia

ISBN: 9781761632976

Cover and text design: George Saad
Front cover image: Tim de Waele / Getty Images
Back cover image: Tina Smigielski

Typeset by Midland Typesetters, Australia
Printed and bound in Australia by Griffin Press

 The paper this book is printed on is certified against the Forest Stewardship Council® Standards. Griffin Press holds chain of custody certification SCS-COC-001185. FSC® promotes environmentally responsible, socially beneficial and economically viable management of the world's forests.

To Kai, who showed me and continues to show me giving up isn't an option

FOREWORD

FOREWORD

I first met Saya in 2019, just a few months before I was welcomed warmly into her family home as host of *Better Homes and Gardens* to do a profile piece on the 'BMX Siblings' – Kai and Saya. The two of them had shot some gorgeous hero interviews for the Tokyo Olympic Games for Seven Sport.

I'd been called immediately at the conclusion of that shoot by one of my producers. Everyone who had dealt with them was completely captivated. They couldn't stop raving about them – this incredible brother and sister duo, both articulate, both ferocious competitors, both great prospects for the upcoming Olympics . . . and they both had Australian and Japanese heritage, representing Australia at an Olympics held in Japan. It was a story with lots of layers to it. The type of story you dream of, where no matter which way you decide to tell it, there's something that will hook viewers. It was a no-brainer that we'd showcase them. With their hectic racing and travel schedules, we shot the story many months before we planned to air it, closer to the Games.

They were as delightful as we'd hoped they would be. Kai was extremely confident, with a passion for reading sports biographies, and anything psychology related, in his quest to gain a competitive edge. Saya was definitely shyer, less willing to make bold statements about what the future may hold for her. You sensed she was a little less sure of herself. She was still a dream to work with, but it was clear she wasn't calling a lot of the shots when it came to her sport. The camera absolutely loved both of them, and as they started to relax and have fun on the day, we knew without a doubt our audience would fall instantly in love with them.

Sadly, we never got to air that story, as Kai suffered a severe and traumatic brain injury in a race accident early the following year, an accident which changed his and his family's lives in an instant. One thing was blindingly clear, though: this tight-knit family were going to rally. Rally for Kai, for themselves and for each other.

Then, during the delayed Tokyo Olympics held in 2021, I was co-hosting Seven's coverage of the Games, and like our viewers at home, watched on in horror as Saya crashed while in the lead during the semi-final. She was carried off unconscious on a stretcher. I honestly thought I was going to be sick. Our hearts went out to the whole Sakakibara family who'd been watching (we even had cameras on Yuki and Kai at Yuki's mother's house in Japan as part of our coverage), as the trauma of two years prior came crashing back like a freight train.

Thirty minutes later we were relaying the news that Saya had been 'medically cleared'. It's an interesting label, that – being 'medically cleared' – because it makes you automatically think someone is one hundred per cent okay. But concussions don't often work like that.

FOREWORD

A few months after the Tokyo Games, *Better Homes and Gardens* returned to makeover the backyard of the Sakakibara's Sydney home, in an attempt to make it more accessible for the whole family, and particularly for Kai.

It was then, while interviewing Saya, that I got a real understanding of the unbelievable and relentless silent battle she'd gone through after several concussions. She was exhausted, still talking about her racing career but with none of the spark I'd come to know.

We know so much more about severe concussions these days and how debilitating they can be. But to see and hear from Saya what she'd been through was quite confronting. A silent condition is very hard for people to truly understand what you are going through.

While it was obvious that her confidence had taken a real battering, Saya is a rare breed. She has an inner strength and steely calmness about her that can honestly give you goosebumps when you talk to her. She can sometimes almost come off as quite intense. But she is also incredibly willing to learn and work on herself.

It's not until you read this book that you get an incredibly honest and personal insight into just how methodical, dedicated and persistent she has had to be to reclaim her self-belief, her self-confidence and her passion for her sport.

I, like many others, watched her heroics in Paris while

absolutely bawling my eyes out. Tears of happiness and relief for her, and her family. I was equal parts proud of her and in awe of her.

Along the way, she's come into her own. Through the trials and tribulations that life has put her through, she's come out triumphant on the other side.

I watch with a smile on my face these days at how relatable Saya is when she speaks in interviews, and I love seeing how confident and inspiring she is to crowds of adoring audiences. She has always been a class act, but now she is a lot more comfortable with the attention that comes her way.

Saya has been through much more than most, but boy it's been an absolute joy to watch her mature as an athlete, and a woman. And I just love the fact she's happy to share all her strengths and more importantly, her vulnerabilities, so that people can really get an honest perspective into what it really takes to reach the pinnacle in sport that she has achieved.

Johanna Griggs
Network Seven presenter and former Australian swimmer

PROLOGUE

This is it. Everything I've trained for. The fears I've faced and the sacrifices I've made all boil down to this moment.

I'm finally at the Olympic Games.

As I walk up the back of the start hill for my race, I feel the hard thumping of my heart in my chest. I feel the nervous energy from the nearby racers, like a heavy cloud around me. But I try not to think about them.

Nothing matters right now but me and what I'm doing. Thinking about my opponents is just a distraction.

My legs feel tired and sluggish as I reach the top of the steep incline. At the top of the eight-metre-high start hill, I can see the impressive BMX racing track in front of me. The hill, the coloured corners and the grandstands. It's a spectacular sight. I take another deep breath to calm my nerves, remembering a piece of advice from my long-time idol Sarah Walker, the silver medallist at London 2012 for BMX racing and a legend in the sport.

She told me: 'Remember to look around, take in your surroundings and remind yourself of how cool it is that you get to be here.' Her words of wisdom whisk away the nerves for a moment, but not for long. They're soon back, along with a flood of negative thoughts.

I'm going to miss the gate. The other girls are faster than me. What happens if I crash?

JUST GO

Everyone is watching.

I shake my head in an attempt to clear my thoughts. I force my mind to focus on the present moment and the cue my coach says to me: 'Just go.'

When I'm about to race at such an important event, there is no space in my mind to think about the technical stuff. For example, *Relax my arms, remember to pedal four times.* Everything to do with my performance should now be instinctual from the hours and hours of physical and mental preparation. There should be no thinking. Just telling yourself to do what you've trained to do.

There is a huge trust element to it. 'Just go' means to trust my preparation and trust that my body knows what to do.

It's the only task left.

Doubts? *Just go.*

There's wind? *Just go.*

It's a mantra I've always come back to, to keep me focused on what I need to do and filter out everything else.

My past races, how I feel, what I think, all irrelevant.

Just go.

I stand up tall and I begin to feel confident as I roll to the gate. I am in lane one, the most inside lane and where I feel the most comfortable – and in my opinion, the most advantageous. I know if I nail my start, I can get out in front and control the race from there.

PROLOGUE

> **JUST GO. IT'S A MANTRA I'VE ALWAYS COME BACK TO**

JUST GO

The announcer starts to call out the name of each rider on the gate. One by one, the broadcast crew pushes a camera up close to each competitor's face. Some wave, some give a stoic look of confidence, some ignore the camera completely.

I am last to get my name called out, '... and from Australia, Saya Sakakibara.' I wave to the camera and as I put my hands back onto the handlebars, I look at the tight yellow jersey covering my arms. The feeling of the stretchy fabric, snug on my body, reminds me that I'm ready to go fast – very fast – even my uniform is designed to be aerodynamic.

'Set,' calls the gate starter. I prepare to react.

The start of every BMX race is the same. There is always a call that says: 'Okay, riders. Random start. Riders ready. Watch the gate.'

After the word 'gate', there are four beeps in quick succession. The gate drops on the fourth beep. But the tricky thing is that between the word 'gate' and that very first beep could be any stretch of time between half a second and three seconds. It's completely random. You never know. You have to be ready to react in an instant – that's part of the competition.

Just go, I silently remind myself.

'Riders ready, watch the gate.'

I wait. Focused.

The gate goes down and I nail my start. I race down the hill and I let my body take over, soaring over the jumps, pedalling hard, fighting to get in front by the first corner.

PROLOGUE

I turn and head for the second straight. I'm leading.

I'm aggressive, racing like a bunny rabbit trying to make some distance away from the rest of the pack. This is my moment.

I turn the second corner and tell myself, *I'm halfway*. Then I notice the aching in my legs. They're screaming at me to stop but I don't listen, pedalling at full speed towards the next set of jumps.

Except my legs are now pedalling in squares. *What?* They aren't turning smoothly. I'm struggling. I clear the first jump but it's like my legs have switched off.

I'm slowing down. A huge sense of panic sets in. *Go faster, Saya!*

I launch into the air as I attempt to clear the next jump. Then I feel a hit from behind, taking me completely off balance.

There's no way to adjust. I'm headed straight for the dirt and I brace for impact.

Everything goes black.

Yes, that wasn't the Olympic Games story of gold medal glory you might have been expecting. Some people probably forget that before Paris 2024, before that picture-perfect victory made headlines, I'd had my hopes dashed in the most horrific circumstances in Tokyo in 2021.

But here we are. And if there's one thing I've learnt over the painful past few years, after tumbling down to the absolute depths of despair and clawing my way back out again, it's that without these bad moments, there can never be any good.

You don't get to have one without the other – they are linked, intertwined like the Olympic rings. All part of the same universe and totally inescapable.

It's just that on that miserable day in Tokyo, I had no idea just how many bad moments were still to come.

I thought the universe had thrown just about everything it could at me. But it was only the beginning.

CHAPTER ONE

THE DAY EVERYTHING CHANGED

He'll be fine. He's always fine.

It was 2020, a year and a half before the Tokyo Games were held. The UCI BMX World Cup began early in the year to avoid clashing with the Olympics. Of course, no one knew yet that the pandemic would delay the Olympics a whole year. Things kicked off in Australia. It was exciting because it'd been about a decade since they were last staged down under.

My brother Kai and I were stoked. Both professional BMX riders, we'd been travelling all around the world together for these World Cups for the last two years. Finally they were going to be on home turf.

BMX racing is like sprinting on two wheels. Each race is a short, high-speed sprint around a dirt track filled with jumps, turns and rhythm sections – those back-to-back bumps that riders pump through instead of pedalling. It's fast, intense and packed with action from the very start. It's not just about pedalling as hard as possible. If you don't have precision, flow, skill, and a whole lot of guts, you've got no chance.

If you've ever watched a race, you know how wild it can be. Riders launching off a massive start hill, flying over jumps, and diving into corners, all while battling seven others for the best position. And all of this happens in less than a minute.

Sounds simple, right?

You go from zero to fifty-five kilometres per hour in about

two-and-a-half seconds. From there, it's a battle of power, technique and split-second decisions. There are no lanes from start to finish.

It's a total free-for-all in which you can go left, right, wherever you want. And then, after thirty to forty seconds, the race is over. It requires all of the body's capabilities.

It's exhilarating, full of adrenaline, and ever since we were kids, Kai and I have been obsessed with it.

Our first stop of the World Cup that year was Shepparton in regional Victoria, and then a week later, competition moved to Bathurst in New South Wales, a few hours north-west of Sydney. World Cups are an important, annual series held over the course of the year, with rounds held in different parts of the world – usually in Europe and the USA. They are always held over a weekend. On a Saturday, riders like myself compete in the qualifying round, semi-final and final (assuming they make it that far) and do it all again on the Sunday. Each day, competitors collect points based on their finishing place. At the end of the year, the person with the most points is crowned World Cup champion.

Besides the Olympic Games, another prestigious event is the World Championships that are held every year. This is different to the World Cups mainly because this is one full day of racing, where the winner of the final is the world champion. The names are confusing, I know. But bear with me.

You would think that being World Cup champion would have more prestige to it, since to win it you have to be consistent throughout the whole year. But strangely, being a world champion is considered more prestigious, because the winner gets to wear the 'rainbow jersey' – a white jersey with rainbow stripes on it. This signifies that they are the world champion, and it's the same in other cycling disciplines under the Union Cycliste Internationale (UCI).

Winning a World Cup race was still something Kai and I aspired to. And, especially, we dreamt of winning in front of a home crowd.

Over the Christmas holidays, Kai and I spent a lot of time driving back and forth to the track in Bathurst – almost every weekend. It gave us the chance to practise and get really familiar with the conditions. After all, no two BMX tracks are the same.

We figured by the time we raced on it for real, we'd know it like the back of our hands. We would absolutely smoke the competition.

We made a couple of trips to Shepparton too, but Bathurst was much closer to where we lived, so we made good use of the proximity and became quasi-locals that summer.

Shepparton came around and we both felt ready for it. It was so cool to have both my parents there watching. I did quite well that weekend, finishing second and fourth. Even though I didn't

THE DAY EVERYTHING CHANGED

win, I felt an immense sense of achievement because I'd felt a lot of pressure to perform in front of my friends and family, and I was able to ride my best despite it. Racing in front of a home crowd was like no other experience I'd had. Having the loudest cheers from the crowd felt so special.

Kai, on the other hand, didn't have the best of weekends, missing out on the final on both days. It wasn't until the next day that we got the chance to debrief as we packed up the car for the seven-hour drive home.

Kai was fast, capable, skilful and the hardest worker I knew. He'd made multiple World Cup finals, became an Australian and Oceania champion, and proven himself to be one of the best BMX racers in the world. The downside to his determination is the deep introspection he had. Sometimes, it would cause him to overthink ahead of a race.

Because of this, I watched him fall short of what he really was capable of countless times. It broke my heart every time.

I felt his heartbreak as he spoke to me about his feelings after the racing in Shepparton. Kai was driving and I was in the passenger seat. He spoke to me while keeping his eyes on the road the whole time. He was so hard on himself. I remember the frustration in his voice, beating himself up about not being able to perform at the level he knew he could. But this conversation felt heavier than usual. Kai was now worried about not earning the results he needed to qualify for the Tokyo Olympic Games; to be on the Australian Olympic Team.

I remember telling him it wasn't over yet, that he was good enough.

'You have to trust yourself, and just go,' I said.

Our next opportunity came a week later at Bathurst. A lot of people racing that weekend felt the pressure, including Kai and me. Depending on how well Australia did as a country, there were either one or two spots in the Olympic team up for grabs among the men. If Kai wanted one of them, he'd really have to do well.

One of the big things we had learnt from our training sessions in Bathurst was that it could get very windy. It was really intense at times. And when you're racing, wind can be a real problem. If the wind is blowing the same direction as the track, it's either going to give you a boost from behind or slow you down from in front. This is usually manageable. But it gets dangerous when there's a crosswind. If it's strong enough, wind can catch the riders mid-jump and throw them off balance, shooting them right off their bikes.

As we settled into the Team Australia Airbnb for the week, I opened up my weather app on my phone. The weather was looking pretty hairy for the weekend. It was the talk of the town among the riders. The wind was strong during the practice sessions before the race, meaning a lot of the riders weren't able

THE DAY EVERYTHING CHANGED

to ride the track properly. By the day of the race, the wind hadn't eased, then the rain started. Conditions were so gross. Wet. Windy. The absolute worst environment to race in. But that's BMX; it's an outdoor sport and the weather conditions are simply part of racing. Me and Kai were determined to make the most out of the opportunity even if the conditions weren't on our side.

Each race, there are officials in charge of safety, who look at the weather and other factors that might make a particular event more dangerous. They have the power to make changes or even cancel the race in response to bad weather. For example, they can make the riders launch off a five-metre hill, which is usually used by amateur riders, instead of the standard eight-metre one, which the elites race off. This makes the race a bit safer because riders don't have to jump the first jump, making it less likely that they'll get caught by the wind.

Despite the conditions, the decision was made to push ahead that day, with riders starting off the five-metre hill, but with no other changes.

Not everyone agreed with the decision to continue racing. In hindsight, I think it was too dangerous and perhaps the officials misjudged the weather risks. There were even a few riders who 'rolled' the race as a way of protesting. Essentially, they rode the lap very slowly.

Kai was in the final group of men to race. I was in the second group of women. So, I was just behind the start hill getting myself ready when he took off. In BMX, men and women both race on the same track. However, most tracks on the international circuit split the track for certain sections. The men's side has bigger jumps, usually ones with gaps in the middle – imagine a take-off ramp and a landing ramp. The women's side has smaller jumps that are not so demanding. It's not a requirement for the women to jump – but it could be an advantage if they do.

I was in staging behind the start hill, sitting on my bike with the other women in my race. There's never much chitchat. Everyone is focused on themselves. I could feel the fierce wind howl by me, the cold, damp air seeping into my racing gear.

Ordinarily, I don't watch other races when I'm in the zone, especially Kai's races. I want to stay focused on what I need to do. I need my mind to be clear and controlled. But at the Bathurst track, there was a giant screen that was just off to the side of me playing the racing live. As I was waiting, I could see everything.

Everything.

I don't know what happened. I still don't understand how it transpired. But on the second straight, Kai went down. It looked really brutal. It took my breath away to see it happen, and in that instant, I knew it was a bad crash. You could instantly feel the atmosphere in the whole venue shift.

He'll be fine, I thought to myself. *He's always fine.*

THE DAY EVERYTHING CHANGED

Over the course of his career, Kai had crashed more times than I could count. He'd had some pretty gnarly injuries too. But he always turned out okay. That's just the guy he is. I think he wore a few of those battle scars on his muscular frame like proud mementoes. He was aggressive and fast, and sometimes he crashed. That's just how it goes, and he was far from unique in that respect – this is a high-octane sport.

I quickly looked away from the screen. I didn't want to watch and become distracted right before I had to race. And besides, I figured he'd get up, limp to the medical tent, maybe be sent to hospital if he'd broken something, and that would be that.

I wasn't worried. In fact, I was totally focused on trying to get my mind back to mentally preparing for my race. But it was hard to ignore the lump I felt in the pit of my stomach.

It must've been at least five minutes before I looked up at the screen again. I couldn't help myself. *Holy crap.* He still hadn't gotten up. He wasn't moving. There were a team of medical personnel hovering over him, blocking the camera's view. I could feel eyes on me, so I tried to stay perfectly calm. I concentrated on controlling my facial expression and taking quiet, deep breaths to steady myself. I didn't want anyone to worry. There was no reason to worry.

He'll be fine. He's always fine.

After a while, it became clear that the racing was put on pause for the time being. I took my helmet off and parked my bike at the team pit area. There was a lot of uncertainty in the air. The rain had stopped but the wind was still howling. Will the racing still go ahead? Is Kai okay?

Then I heard a helicopter in the distance. The whoop-whoop-whoop of its blades got closer and closer, until it landed next to the track. Kai was loaded in with our mum by his side.

I don't know how much time had passed by now – maybe thirty or forty minutes. Maybe longer, it was hard to tell. But Dad had come to find me. He said he was going to drive to the hospital and meet Kai and Mum there.

That's when he told me.

'Kai's stopped breathing,' he said.

There was this look in Dad's eyes. He was petrified.

But Dad's palpable fear had the opposite effect on me. It made me display confidence; a determination that Kai was going to be just fine.

'Okay,' I replied. I said it assertively, reassuringly, as if to say to Dad: *Stop freaking out.*

I had to stay. I assumed racing would continue after the helicopter cleared the track. And I had another race the next morning, after all. Both races were very important in determining if I was going to the Tokyo Olympic Games in a few months' time.

The Olympic Games.

THE DAY EVERYTHING CHANGED

> **BMX IS HIGH STAKES. IT'S EXTREME**

JUST GO

My Dad didn't know what to say or do. He wished me luck before he disappeared into the crowd.

It didn't feel like a wrong or weird decision to stay at the time. I had to think about me, and Kai had always been fine before. Why would this be any different?

After what felt like hours of waiting, the rest of the day's racing was cancelled because the wind wasn't easing up. The organisers asked some of the riders to stick around to do an autograph session for the fans that had come to watch. I was smiling and going about my business as usual.

When people asked me, 'Is Kai okay?' or, 'Have you heard any news on Kai?' I responded with a smile.

'He's had better days.'

It must be so hard for people outside of the sport to understand, but BMX racing is high stakes. It's extreme. I mean, there's a reason why Red Bull sponsors BMX racing athletes. It's fast, heart-pumping and action-filled. Crashes happen. We all know and accept that.

There was no real reason, based on what I knew, for me to suspect that Kai wasn't going to fully recover.

I was sad for him, though. Not about Kai's crash as such, but about the stark reality that his Olympic dream was over. There was no way he was going to be able to qualify for Tokyo now.

That's where my mind was. On what this meant for his goals. On how devastated he was going to feel in the morning.

THE DAY EVERYTHING CHANGED

I thought *that* would be the heaviest blow to my best friend and training partner.

My boyfriend Romain, or Rom as I call him, is also a BMX racer, and had flown from his home country of France for the race. I went back to his room that afternoon to watch Netflix and pass the time.

My phone buzzed with messages asking how Kai was. I got phone calls asking for updates every hour. I simply didn't comprehend that this was serious.

'He's at Canberra Hospital, but I don't know much more than that,' I would reply.

'I'm sure he'll be fine,' I told them.

I had no idea.

It was barely seven o'clock the next morning when I awoke to a call from my dad. He was at the hospital in Canberra. I had never heard him sound like that. Shaken. Terrified. On the verge of tears. It sent chills throughout my body.

'Kai's going in for brain surgery,' he said. 'I think you should come here.'

A sense of numbness washed over me and then I started panicking. I threw clothes into my bag, my chest heaving with sobs.

My dad didn't say much else, but it was clear that Kai wasn't okay.

Dad had phoned my coach and asked if someone could drive me to Canberra, knowing that I would probably not be in a state to get myself there.

I really don't remember too much about the journey. My coach had arranged for a friend called Chris to drive me the three hours to Canberra. We had only just met that week.

The journey was silent; punctuated just by the sound of my sobbing and sniffing. The only time I spoke was two minutes into the drive when I asked Chris to make a quick stop at the motel where Rom was staying.

I had messaged him letting him know I was coming. When he opened the door, I fell into his arms and cried.

'He's never going to be the same,' I sobbed into his shoulder. He held me tightly, not knowing what to do or say.

I didn't want to leave Rom. I wanted him by my side. I needed him. I didn't want to go to Canberra. I didn't want this to be real. I wanted to wake up from this nightmare, but I couldn't.

The air felt heavy in the car. When I looked outside the window to see the scenery flash by, even the sky was downcast and looming. The country road was empty, like how I felt inside.

Was the weather to blame for Kai's crash? I tried to dissect the whole situation from the start, to understand it better. The wind was certainly a consideration; what about the condition of the track? What did I remember seeing on the screen?

THE DAY EVERYTHING CHANGED

I couldn't figure it out. I still don't know. I've played it over in my mind again and again and I can't land on a definite reason. For it not to be obvious, like clipping another rider or landing awkwardly from a jump, is so bizarre. Whatever the cause, the outcome was horrific. Kai went headfirst into the asphalt.

I guess I had hoped that by the time I got to Canberra things would be different. That whatever had necessitated Kai's surgery was fixed and the outlook was suddenly positive.

My brother would be sitting up in bed, looking sheepish and telling me to get back to Bathurst as quickly as possible to not miss my race.

But that was not how it was – at all. As we pulled up at the hotel next to the hospital, my parents came into view. I will never forget the look on their faces – it quickly reminded me of reality. They were devastated. I've never seen them look so small and vulnerable.

'Kai should be out of surgery soon,' Dad said. 'They don't know whether he's going to make it, or anything. We just have to wait.'

I looked over at Mum in the hopes that perhaps Dad was joking. But the emotion on her face told me this was real. I don't know whether it was exhaustion from the crying in the car or just being in a state of shock, but I felt numb. Completely emotionless.

I followed my parents as they navigated through the hospital halls to the ICU, and we arrived just as Kai was getting wheeled out of surgery.

I didn't recognise him. His face was so swollen. He was bald. He was hooked up to a ventilator. He looked frail. There were so many tubes and cords connected to almost every part of his body.

Strong. Smart. Fearless. That's who Kai was for his entire life, and how I viewed him a mere twenty-four hours earlier. Now, here he was, lying helplessly in a hospital bed, barely clinging to life. *Is this even real? What the hell is happening?* It felt like a nightmare, totally surreal.

Would he wake up? Would he walk again? Would he ever be able to speak again? The doctors couldn't tell us anything. It was so frustrating because we were so desperate for any kind of indication of his future. But it was too early to tell. The neurosurgeons were doing damage control at this point, focused on keeping his heart beating. Although, they did say they were satisfied with the result of the operation.

I wish they had more answers, I'd think. But then we were shown his MRI.

As the doctor explained to me and my parents what the scan illustrated, I thought I was going to throw up. The damage to his brain was significant and his body had been battered very badly. There was so much pressure and swelling in his brain caused by a very serious bleed. The bleed was right in the middle of his head, so there was no easy way of getting access to it to drain the blood out. The only option was to remove a piece of his skull. This would create room for the brain to swell without damaging any more parts of the brain.

I was panicking. I watched my dad walk away – he was absolutely distraught, unable to watch the images any longer. It's a state I'd never seen him in. He's strong and in control and stoic at all times. Seeing this formerly unseen side of him really rattled me.

'Mum, we're going to lose him, aren't we?' I asked.

She shook her head defiantly. 'No, it's not over for Kai yet. I know it.'

It was a statement of fact. Not a hope, not a plea to God. It was a mixture of her assessment of the situation along with the reality she was absolutely confident would eventuate. I clung to those words and her rigid belief that he was going to come out the other side.

I was distressed, shaken, untethered. I sat in the room, watching him, unable to fathom the scene before me.

He looked dead. The way he was positioned in that bed, pale, tangled in wires and tubes, made it look like he'd already left us. A shell kept alive by machines that hummed and beeped. Just over twenty-four hours ago, we were having oats for breakfast together. He was hogging the peanut butter and I was swatting at his hand, laughing, trying to get one decent scoop. *And now he's here.* Was he here? At least his body was. But Kai, the brother I knew, was nowhere to be found.

It perhaps sounds strange, but in that moment I got my phone out and started recording. Landscape. I knew that this was day one of the journey. I thought that maybe one day there'd be a documentary on Kai's miraculous recovery. As I was recording, I wished so badly that it was five years in the future; that my brother had totally recovered and we were no longer living this horrific reality.

> 9 FEBRUARY 2020
> Canberra, Australia
>
> In my entire life, twenty whole years, that was the first time I saw my dad cry.
>
> It absolutely broke my heart. It actually hurt my chest. It hit me that this is our reality.
>
> Kai is really badly injured. He might not wake up. He might never be the same again.

As Mum, Dad and I left the hospital on that first day, my phone vibrated. It was news that day two of racing was also cancelled due to the weather. Attached to the notification was a photo of all the BMX riders at Bathurst standing on the start hill, arranged to spell out 'K', 'A' and 'I'. They made heart shapes with their hands. They were smiling.

The riders in the photo looked so happy. It wasn't a photo taken with sympathy in mind – but with a sense that this was a blip and Kai would be fine sooner rather than later.

I realised those riders didn't know. They had no idea how bad things were because suddenly this was our world, and we were the only ones living in it.

Out there, Kai had crashed but was going to be fine. In here, he was in a coma and no one really knew for sure what was going to happen next.

Whenever my mind drifted to a scary place, I remembered my mum's reassuring words. This wasn't his time. We'd deal with what came next when it rose to meet us.

CHAPTER TWO

NO TRAINING WHEELS

I was nine and Kai was twelve when we first declared we would race in the Olympic Games.

BMX racing had been added as an Olympic sport and we sat in the living room, our faces pressed to the television screen, so close our noses almost touched it. We were so utterly absorbed.

'How awesome would it be?' Kai said, sighing.

'Would what be?'

'Going to the Olympics. Winning a gold medal. Being the champion of champions.'

It actually hadn't dawned on me until he said it. I guess because it hadn't been a possibility until then. It just wasn't on my radar – but it was firmly on his.

That declaration would end up being a dream we'd share together. The direction in which we were headed. It always starts with a dream.

My mum, Yuki, is Japanese, and my dad, Martin, is English. They met in Sydney in the 1990s, fell in love, got married and were settled on the Gold Coast by the time Kai and I came along.

I was born in Tallebudgera, Gold Coast, Australia, but when I was two years old, my family moved to Japan. Both Mum and Dad's Aussie visas expired and they spent some time tossing up where to head to: England or Japan. Mum's homeland won out, and so off we went. We lived in the suburbs of Tokyo for almost six years.

NO TRAINING WHEELS

I was a pretty normal Japanese kid. Japanese was actually my first language. I went to school, I played with my friends. I participated in typical Japanese customs like Shichi-Go-San (translated to Seven-Five-Three), where three, five and seven-year-old children dress in kimonos and visit temples and shrines to make offerings. Even though I may have looked a little different to the other kids around me, it didn't bother me. I felt right at home, where I belonged.

Around the time I was seven, my parents decided to move back to Australia. They missed it much more than they enjoyed Japan, so they sorted out new visas and began preparing to uproot us.

Kai had fallen in love with BMX just before my family left Australia. Back in 2001 he got a bike with Batman on it for Christmas. He was three and once he got on, he essentially never got off again.

As luck would have it, there was a BMX track right next to the preschool he went to in Ashmore on the Gold Coast. Mum and Dad took him along one day and the obsession took hold.

As the years passed, Kai's love for the sport never waned. He was super into it. Mum and Dad would practically have to drag him off the track at the end of the day. He rode so much and loved it so much.

When it came to riding a bike, my dad didn't believe in training wheels. His philosophy was that you should learn how to balance first and then turn your mind to the pedals, not the other way around. So, when he bought me my first bike, a little chrome GT, he took the pedals off altogether. I would push it around, teetering from side to side, getting used to balancing my weight on it. Once I got the hang of it, he put the pedals back on, and I was on my way.

I didn't really think much about whether I liked BMX or not. I don't have much memory of starting out. But I think I just wanted to be like my big brother. And this was his world. His entire world. It didn't really matter if I loved it. I was happy to tag along.

I feel sorry for Kai when I think back now about how annoying I must have been. He was my older brother, so I wanted to be wherever he was. As soon as I could walk, I was always only a few steps behind him.

In 2007, when I was about to turn eight years old, I was so excited to move to Australia. I wasn't too sad about leaving the only place I knew as home, about saying goodbye to my friends and heading somewhere strange and mysterious. In fact, I couldn't wait – I was eager for an adventure.

I might've been young, but I knew a thing or two about the country. To me, it was this quirky but friendly land of blue skies, clean air and wide-open spaces. For an outdoors-loving kid, it was a dream come true. Long stretches of pristine beaches to run on, thick bushland to explore. Endless fun awaited.

We settled in Helensburgh, a small town about halfway between Sydney and Wollongong, just south of the picturesque Royal National Park. It was a perfect place to call home.

On paper, it should've sucked. I didn't speak English and knew I had to learn it fast. I was an outsider. But I felt nothing but welcomed. Everyone at my new school was so nice. I made friends quickly. And I picked up my second language in a short amount of time. Dad says Kai and I had an Aussie accent within a month.

Another thing that helped me settle in was immediately getting stuck into BMX. Compared to Japan, Australia felt like BMX heaven. Kai's school friends all owned BMX bikes, unlike in Japan, where the kids owned town bikes. Kai and his friends spent their afternoons around the bush tracks of Helensburgh, building jumps and tearing through the trails. I tagged along sometimes.

Not to mention that there were five BMX tracks within an hour-and-a-half drive of home. There were more if we drove a little further. Compared to the grand total of seven tracks in the whole of Japan that we were used to, this was paradise. We could go to a different track every weekend.

We signed up to our local BMX club, Southlake Illawarra BMX Club in Albion Park. It was about forty minutes' drive from our place. Our parents drove us down every Wednesday night for open training and every Friday night for club racing. And on a Sunday morning, we would wake up at the crack of dawn and head to another BMX track to practise.

There's no denying Kai loved BMX way more than me. He was more obsessed with the sport. He was excited to train every single time, whereas I was excited when it rained and we couldn't go. He drew bikes on his schoolbooks, had pictures of his favourite riders covering every inch of his bedroom wall, and watched DVD compilations of races nonstop. He lived and breathed it. So, each of these training sessions was led by Kai's desire. It wasn't something that I was itching to do, but I was good at it and I enjoyed it while I was there.

Around our house in Helensburgh was lots of thick bushland, where kids in years gone by had carefully carved out these trails and mounds. We'd tear through on our bikes and try to tackle these crude homemade jumps.

The jumps had nothing in the middle – just a take-off and a landing, so you had to fully commit. You couldn't change your mind at the last second and roll over them. You'd wind up hurtling headfirst into the dirt. Though they scared me, and were a type of jump I would never see on an official track, it was still good practice that helped me develop my BMX skills.

NO TRAINING WHEELS

I always felt a flurry in my stomach and a tightening around my heart when I did these dirt jumps. Kai would do it without a second thought. I would dread the days Kai would drag me out there, because it meant I had to face my fears.

Jumping on the BMX track was different. There was a middle to those, meaning you had the option of rolling over it if you wanted. I felt safer when I had that choice. I could go fast and get air. Yes, it was scary, but as a young girl it also felt so cool that I could do that. It was even better when I tried a jump I'd never done before. I felt fear every time, so I had to have a few practice runs at the new jump until I built up the courage to give it my all. I was always ecstatic when I landed it.

Kai was so driven and he wanted to do absolutely everything possible to be the best at BMX racing. When I was young, I was probably mucking around too much.

Sometimes I'd take the piss out of him for being so serious. I'd wind him up by trying to make him laugh. I thought it was funny, until he'd snap and get angry at me.

'Saya, you're not taking it seriously,' he'd lecture me.

It was pretty typical kid stuff. But we always made up and I'd try extra hard to be as focused as him.

It was evident that I had natural talent, which helped. I picked up techniques and skills really quickly. I think a big reason for that was all the time I spent watching my brother. I tagged along with him to the track, so I got to study him closely. He was always faster, stronger and more skilled than me. And he cared about me a lot so he would push me to try a new jump, or give me different combinations to do, to challenge my skills. From our childhood all the way through our teenage years.

'Saya, jump the triple today,' he would say.

'What triple?' I would respond, knowing full well what triple he was talking about. It was a big jump with three humps. I had conquered the jump that was slightly smaller than this not long ago, and the next challenge was the triple. Usually these are the biggest jumps on a BMX track. I had to go much faster and jump higher if I wanted to clear the whole thing. It was scary. As much as it would be so awesome if I landed it, there was a high risk of crashing if I didn't jump properly.

I didn't want to crash. I hated being hurt. But I knew it was important for me to do it, if I wanted to keep getting better. So I would build up the courage, grip my handlebars tight and with Kai's guidance I would give it a shot. Sometimes I would jump too short, so I'd have to try again. Sometimes I would crash, end up covered head-to-toe in dirt and grazes. But most often, I would clear the jump first go, and come back grinning from ear to ear under my helmet.

And, over time, I learnt how to ride skilfully, like the boys around me that were the same age. Fast. Confident. Flowing. And I soon noticed that I rode better than the girls around me. I was the only girl that was jumping.

NO TRAINING WHEELS

I loved going fast. And I loved winning. I loved being skilful.

There was no greater feeling than beating everyone else. And I wanted to feel it again and again. It was addictive.

But BMX was full of conflicting experiences – I didn't love the feeling of pushing myself to face my fears, but I loved the thrill I got when I did. Some people are born for it, their brains wired to crave fear and challenge. The same way some elite athletes talk about their drive and hunger like it was always part of them. From a young age, I realised that if I wanted to win in this sport, I had to be brave and do those things that scared me.

On the days we went to the track on the weekends to train, my dad would be the one to wake Kai and me up at six in the morning to go ride on a BMX track. I would usually sleep in the car. A lot of BMX racing tracks are open to the public. Although the gate start wouldn't be operating, we could still ride the track and work on our skills.

I'd be nervous because Dad expected the best out of me. He'd push me hard to not only attempt the jumps but to do them well. He would take videos, using a little camcorder, of the whole practice session – every single run Kai and I did. I didn't want to disappoint him. But with the help of Kai's encouragement, I would be brave and attempt new jumps and try to perfect my skills.

By the end of the session, I'd be so excited to get home again to share with Mum what I'd managed to achieve.

> **I LOVED GOING FAST. AND I LOVED WINNING.**

NO TRAINING WHEELS

We'd plug the video camera into the TV and watch the footage back together as a family – the good moments as well as the bad runs.

Our entire lives were BMX. I didn't know any different – I assumed all normal families had some shared interest that everyone obsessively played a part in pursuing.

In BMX, boys and girls have their own separate classes. By the time I was eight, we quickly discovered that there were way more boys in the sport than girls. The field in my age group was pretty thin. So, Dad put me in the boys class.

When I started winning, it was freaking amazing. I loved racing against the boys and I especially loved beating them. It was so good. It became normal. I was the girl always racing the boys. At races, as the announcers called out the names, they'd say: 'Good luck boys . . . and girl.'

Some of the other dads got a bit cranky that their boys were getting smashed by a girl. I'm sure the boys hated it too! My dad thought it was hilarious. So, I kept racing the boys right up until I was sixteen. By the time I was seventeen, I saw some of the fast younger girls also challenging themselves in the boys class. It was so cool to see.

That's not to say it was easy. Travelling the country and the world racing, sometimes I wished I didn't do BMX. What's unique about BMX racing is that it's an all-age sport. From the club level to world level, there is a class for just about any age group. In the annual World Championship event, riders aged between seven and fifty compete within their age group against riders from other nations. If you win that race, you become a world champion of your class.

Kai and I were fortunate enough to go to the World Championships almost every year. In 2006, we travelled to São Paulo, Brazil, where I raced my first World Championships. I raced in the five-to-seven-year girls class, and came second in the world. The winner was a girl from Aruba, who I beat two years later, in 2008. That made me world champion for the nine-year girls class. By 2015, in my last year as a challenge rider, essentially the 'amateur' categories, I had won the World Championships five times.

Within Australia, there is a National Championships event that mimics the World Championships on a smaller scale. Winning the National Championships and World Championships was my goal every year. Which meant a lot of time was spent training and travelling to races. It also meant that I would miss out on birthdays and parties.

Sometimes I wished I was a normal kid, doing normal kid stuff on the weekend. Sometimes I wished I didn't have the pressure to race, to perform my best. I wished I didn't have to keep being brave and progressing my skills. But at the same time it felt wrong not to be doing that.

If I quit the sport I'd have to show up to watch Kai race

anyway, so why not continue with my own competitions? Looking back, I never did BMX for fun. It was always to win.

I didn't always like doing BMX at the time, but I took a lot of satisfaction from achieving something difficult. And each time I did, my confidence grew.

In cycling, the year you turn seventeen, you can either move into the category for seventeen to twenty-four year olds, and remain racing at an amateur level, or move into the Junior Elite class. Junior Elites are only one step below Elite class, which houses the best racers in the world.

In BMX racing, Junior Elites and Elites race off the Olympic standard eight-metre hills, and can also compete in the World Cup series. I wanted to be like the pros I grew up watching and admiring, so it was a no brainer to join Junior Elite. From nineteen onwards, athletes can join the Elite class, racing against the best of the best.

Being a professional BMX racing athlete is a full-time commitment. Riders spend countless hours in the gym building explosive power to launch out of the gate. Then come the sprint sessions – pedalling full speed on flat roads, or downhill or uphill to develop strength and speed. And of course, there are track sessions dedicated to refining start technique and sharpening bike handling skills, to manoeuvre through the track at top speed. Success in BMX isn't just about being strong – it's about being smooth, controlled and incredibly precise.

JUST GO

The best riders make it look effortless, gliding over jumps and flowing through corners – but behind that illusion is years of grit, training and discipline.

That unpredictability is what makes it so exciting to watch – and so awesome to do. Every race is different, and you never know what's going to happen until the very last moment.

That's BMX racing. Pure speed, skill, and adrenaline. There's no room for fear.

In 2018, after graduating high school, there was only one thing I wanted: to turn Elite and chase the dream alongside Kai, who was already racing and travelling the world. He showed me that being a professional BMX racer was possible – and I was determined to follow in his footsteps. I'd come second at the World Championships the year before in the Junior Elite class, which was enough to join the Australian High Performance National Team that Kai was already in.

By now, I had little fear and a calm confidence that I was good enough to match up against top racers.

Where did this confidence come from? I have no idea, but I guess it was something to do with the fact it was my 'rookie' year.

That year, Kai and I spent three months in Europe, chasing the European circuit and the World Cup rounds. It was such a pinch-yourself time in my life. I felt so lucky that I was able to follow my brother, travelling the world to race bikes.

NO TRAINING WHEELS

I was so amazed by the quality of the riders that turned up every race weekend. I couldn't believe that I was in the Elite class, racing against the racers who I'd looked up to since I was a young girl. All I could think of was how much I would improve if I consistently put myself in this high-stakes environment.

During this time, I heavily relied on Kai. When we turned up to new tracks, I would ask his opinion on whether I could jump certain jumps. I asked him for the best race lines and I sought his encouragement when I doubted my abilities.

'You can do it, you know how to jump,' he told me, as I sized up a big ten-metre jump at one track in Italy.

When racing came around, he would tell me things like 'You're looking really good out there,' and 'I think you'll kill it this weekend.'

Sometimes it felt like he knew me better than I did myself. He certainly knew BMX racing better than I did, so I deeply respected his opinion.

For our entire lives, Kai had shown me what hard work looked like. He showed me how to set goals and how to be disciplined enough to achieve them.

Some of my earliest memories are of being in awe of my brother. Like most younger siblings, I looked up to him. He was utterly devoted to BMX racing and becoming the best version of himself. When he was twelve, he begged my parents to get a coach so he could start training. As luck would have it, a former

JUST GO

Australian National Champion, Troy Fisher, lived just up the road from us in Helensburgh. Troy started giving Kai programs, so I joined in too. Troy introduced the idea of keeping a training diary to note down things that went well and things that needed improvement during each session. There was a page in Kai's notebook for every day that he trained. He filled up entire notebooks in no time. Me, on the other hand, my notebooks stayed half finished. I couldn't stay consistent with it, and I didn't really see the benefit.

Kai read books, listened to podcasts and I would see him scribbling down lessons he learned from them. He was always striving, not just to become a better racer but a better person.

In 2018, we created the brand 'Team Sakakibara', which involved making custom race gear, team shirts and we even made YouTube videos of our travels overseas. Kai and I worked together to make a name for ourselves. We tried to do things differently – to reach beyond the BMX community and connect with a wider audience. We dreamed of turning Sakakibara into a household name.

'How cool would it be if we got our names out there and brought more attention to BMX?' Kai would often say.

We constantly dreamed about what we could both achieve together in the sport. We talked about going beyond Olympics, about how to grow the sport and how we could give back to the BMX community. Between competitions we held coaching clinics across Australia and even in Europe, the USA and Japan. We loved connecting with young riders, sharing tips and inspiring the next generation.

When we started working with our manager, Ryan Chipperfield, he helped us get in front of the media to share our story. I was never comfortable in front of a camera, but Kai was a natural. He was just so good at articulating his words. It made me want to get better too.

He didn't just lead our training and plan the logistics of our racing seasons – he took charge of the branding and marketing, too. He was a workhorse, both on and off the bike. Thanks to his relentless drive, we secured sponsors and started gaining real traction towards our dream. We had supporters cheering us on as we shared our vision of going to the Olympics – brother and sister, side by side. We even appeared on a major TV show in Japan.

Kai did so much. And sometimes I just wished I had more to contribute – something that could help our team or support his performance. I often felt like all I was doing was receiving his praise, his encouragement and his advice. And having a big bulk of my racing life taken care of. I felt like I had nothing to give in return. It worried me.

But in 2019, during a joint interview with Channel Seven, Kai said something that stuck with me. It was the 'hero shoot', where they bank a whole lot of footage and content which will be used to profile the athletes, prior to and during the Olympic Games.

In that interview, Kai said that he took a lot of inspiration from me. When I started winning and doing well in my rookie year, he said I showed him what was possible.

If I could do it, so could he.

> **18 NOVEMBER 2019**
> Sydney, Australia
>
> Kai and I went to Channel 7 and did five hours of filming. It was so much fun. The interviews were mostly done as if we were going to the Olympics and had already qualified, even though we don't know yet.
>
> It was another step closer, though and, gosh, it finally clicked! It all seemed so real. I honestly thought we were going together. It was a cool feeling and today was the first time I kind of realised that the whole of Australia is going to get behind us. They are going to remember our names and the support is going to be amazing.

Kai and I trained together, travelled the world together, raced together. When we did signings for fans, it was posters featuring the two of us together that we scribbled our names on.

There was no Saya without Kai. I loved it. I needed it. He was one half of me and so much of my success in BMX was owed to him. There was not a single part of my journey in the sport that didn't feature him in some way.

NO TRAINING WHEELS

The motivator. The cheerleader. The cop. The friend. The training partner. He played so many roles. I couldn't imagine it any other way. I didn't think I'd ever have to.

Until his accident changed everything.

CHAPTER THREE
STEP BY STEP

We booked an Airbnb that was walking distance from the hospital in Canberra, for a month to start with. We had no idea how long our stay was going to be.

Each morning in the days after Kai's crash, Mum, Dad and I would wake at six and quickly get dressed so we could be at the hospital by half-past.

That's when the doctors did their first rounds of the day. We wanted to be able to hear what they said when they assessed Kai's current status.

One of the nurses suggested we keep a diary about Kai's journey, so that when he woke up, he'd have an insight into what had happened while he had been sedated. So, we did. And we wrote it to him. Like: 'Dear Kai, today you had surgery.' That kind of thing. It was part of our daily routine with him.

That nurse also told us that, even though he was in a coma and heavily sedated, she believed that sometimes patients could hear what was going on around them. Maybe he could hear us. She encouraged us to chat with him about anything and everything – keep him company while he recovered.

Kai loved music, so we put his UE Boom speaker by his bed and put his one thousand liked songs on shuffle.

The air around him seemed lighter as the songs played. The nurses enjoyed it and I hoped it brought Kai some positive energy.

STEP BY STEP

I'd read to him every morning. I noticed Kai was reading *That Will Never Work* back at the Airbnb in Bathurst. He always loved to read so I thought I'd start where the bookmark was placed. The author of the book is Marc Randolph, one of the co-founders of Netflix. It's about the sheer persistence, amid struggles and doubts, that turned a fledgling DVD mail rental business into one of the biggest entertainment platforms in the world. At its core, the book is about dedication and being willing to take risks even when people tell you you're crazy.

We got through a chapter together each morning. It felt weird to read to him while his eyes were shut, and he probably didn't hear a single word. But it was nice to focus on something other than how terrified I felt.

11 FEBRUARY 2020
Canberra, Australia

Early wake up.

The visit to the hospital is always the hardest in the morning when we don't know what happened overnight.

Kai's condition could have drastically changed or things could be the same. This time he was the same.

I stayed for about an hour reading to him. Then a nurse started talking to me and asking me questions about BMX. She asked me if I was scared of racing now.

JUST GO

> I was shocked. Honestly, why did she even ask that? It's so freaking dumb.
>
> No, I'm not scared now.

Kai was in a stable but critical condition. It was all very complex, but the doctors and nurses tried their best to explain what was going on. Kai was still heavily sedated in order to give him the best chance to heal. After we were told about it, we were fixated on a particular number on the screen by Kai's bed that indicated the pressure in his brain. Due to the big bleed, there was a lot of swelling, thus causing the pressure, even with that piece of his skull having been removed. The nurses were constantly adjusting his cocktail of medication to keep the pressure down as much as possible. Each day when we walked in, we were either relieved to see the pressure was down, or our chests tightened to see the number had gone up.

A week after the accident, Kai developed pneumonia. His temperature began to rise and now he was fighting an infection. This wasn't helping the swelling in his brain to go down.

The doctors were concerned. It felt like a major setback.

STEP BY STEP

> 15 FEBRUARY 2020
> Canberra, Australia
>
> I really thought it was going to be a constant progress that keeps improving every day, but it's not.
>
> It's up and down. It's frustrating and exhausting.
>
> I hope that tomorrow is another good day.

From the moment I saw Kai in the hospital bed, I knew that it was now up to me to keep our Olympic dream alive.

If he wasn't going to go, then I'm going for the both of us.

We would visit Kai a couple of times a day, staying between fifteen minutes to an hour. There wasn't much we could do but wait the painful days out before we had more answers. That meant I had a lot of free time for the rest of each day.

So, I started a routine, and tried to keep to it as much as possible. That meant continuing to train.

I had the chance to go into the Australian Institute of Sport in Canberra and use their gym. I also had a couple of local BMX tracks nearby that I could ride on.

Training was good, as it was a distraction in some ways, but in others, it was just another reminder of why Kai wasn't there doing heavy squats with me, or why we weren't fighting over whose playlist to blast in the car.

JUST GO

Sometimes I would just let myself cry as I drove myself to training. It was so painful not knowing Kai's outcome.

Most moments, I would be solely in the present. Focusing on myself and doing the training. It's not that I forgot Kai was in hospital, I was just okay with it. And some moments I would be crippled by the very same fact. That we could lose him. I could be doing this alone forever. And I could very well become my parents' only living child.

One day, as I was training, I had a terrible vision. My mind started imagining what it would be like to plan Kai's funeral.

I imagined having to send the terrible texts to the family. Our extended family living around the world were all anxious for answers. I imagined getting ready, dressed in black. I imagined the photo on the order of service. What photo would we use? Who would attend? How big would it be?

I imagined all the sympathetic looks from mourners. The shock, the utter sadness, the dense air that would surround us... It got my heart racing. I was spiralling and tears sprang to my eyes.

This could actually happen. It could be our reality.

I shook my head in an attempt to shake away the sadness.

Stay focused Saya. Kai is going to pull through.

I had to stay strong for Kai. I couldn't let myself fall into darkness. I had to hold on to belief, to those words my mother said.

STEP BY STEP

Not long after this awful vision, and nine days after Kai's crash, we met with Kai's doctors in a standard meeting space tucked away in the corner of the ICU. The small chamber consisted of faux leather couches and a coffee table in the shape of a 'U'. Standard for a hospital. As I entered the room with my mum and dad and waited for the doctors, I wondered how many families had, in this very room, had their hearts ripped out by devastating news.

There was tension in the air as the neurosurgeons carefully chose their words and talked to us about Kai's prognosis. All medical jargon I didn't understand. We just wanted an answer to one question. It was hanging over us, haunting us. We needed to know. My heart thumped as my Dad eventually asked the question.

'Is Kai going to live?' I could hear the emotion in his voice. He was in disbelief that those words just left his mouth.

The doctor's short pause felt like an eternity. I held my breath.

'I think so,' she eventually said. And I know she meant it.

It was an improvement from a week earlier when she said it could go either way.

He was still fighting.

Four days later, I was in the hospital with Kai and I saw him open his eyes a little.

I saw them move, like he was looking around for us. He wasn't responsive, but it gave me this huge jolt of hope that we were on track.

'He's awake!' I shouted. He wasn't really. It turns out coming out of a coma is a slow and unpredictable process. It was only the start of months of 'waking up'.

I don't know why I figured that it would be a lightbulb moment, like waking up in the morning or flicking a switch. Probably from dumb Hollywood movies that make it seem so simple. It wasn't like that for us. I don't think it is for most people.

I soon found out that opened eyes aren't necessarily a sign that a coma is about to end. But it was a small milestone.

> **20 FEBRUARY 2020**
> Canberra, Australia
>
> This morning we saw Kai cough, take a few breaths and we also saw his hand move. Omg. We were all so happy.

Gradually, Kai progressed. He began to look at us; he moved his mouth; he wriggled his finger a little. We were truly overjoyed.

Eventually, he won the fight against pneumonia. Then it was time for the doctors to slowly reduce his sedation. This was a moment of truth for us, because we would find out if he could breathe on his own or not.

There were smiles on our faces when we found Kai lying in the bed one day without being attached to the ventilator, his eyes open and breathing on his own again. What a relief.

STEP BY STEP

The day they moved him out of intensive care was another huge leap forward. It was six weeks after his crash. He was breathing on his own, he was opening his eyes, but there was still a heap of work to do. He had survived. He was alive. He just needed time and we'd take it step by step.

It took me a while to come to terms with our new reality. He had lost twenty kilos of his body weight. A body that took years to build, shrivelled down to skin and bone in just a month. And it was clear that the right side of his body was paralysed – just as the doctors had predicted. He couldn't speak. And I realised I had started to forget what his voice sounded like. He was able to move his left arm to hold my hand. We were even able to play catch with a ball while he was lying down.

That's good that he can see!

I just couldn't imagine how Kai was going to tackle these huge, absolutely mammoth challenges ahead. He was virtually starting from scratch, relearning how to talk and walk – and that was just the tip of the iceberg.

21 MARCH 2020
Canberra, Australia

Seeing Kai today was kind of tough. He was in a single room all alone. He looked so sad. So lonely and bored.

It was cool to see more progress, and I was able to communicate with him through yes or no questions. I asked:

> 'Squeeze my hand for yes. Can you hear me?' Yes.
> 'Do you know who I am?' Yes.
> 'Do you know your name?' No.
> 'Do you get lonely?' Yes.
> 'Do you want your friends to come see you?' No.
> 'Do you want Mum to come see you?' Yes . . .
>
> He's so thin. He looks unhealthily thin and it's so scary. It just reminds me of a sick person dying and it's so heartbreaking. I swear it's harder seeing him now than when he was in ICU.

After Kai began squeezing my hand, I found a piece of paper in the Airbnb where we were staying. On it Dad wrote the words 'yes' and 'no' in bright pink highlighter.

We figured that if Kai could communicate through squeezing my hand, maybe he could eventually point to words too. With this piece of paper, we started to ask questions and communicate with him for the first time.

This was huge, considering not long ago we didn't even know whether he would make it or not.

Although having this communication with Kai was huge, it wasn't completely reliable. The answers to his yes and no questions sometimes contradicted one another and it was hard to understand exactly what he was feeling.

Just over seven weeks after Kai's crash, the missing part of his skull was put back in, and he was transferred to Liverpool Brain Injury Rehabilitation Unit, or BIRU for short. This was a

STEP BY STEP

key milestone. The many harrowing weeks in Canberra Hospital had come to an end, but the start of the gruelling next chapter was just beginning.

Despite the progress, I remember an undeniable truth washing over me.

The brother I knew and loved – the one I knew so well, probably better than anyone else in the world – was gone.

For so long all I wished for was another conversation with him.

---

3 APRIL 2020
Helensburgh, Australia

I got really sad this morning. I had a dream that Kai could speak. Hearing his voice was so amazing and I loved talking to him, asking him questions, hearing about the experience from his perspective.

Then I woke up. That wasn't my reality.

I don't know where that dream came from. I guess I'm feeling really lonely. I get to talk to Kai every day, but he can't talk back. He was my best friend in the whole world – the person who knew me better than anyone else.

We were constantly around each other. We'd have big deep and meaningful chats or just talk about nothing at all. He made me laugh and we used to do so much together that made me happy. He would listen to my problems. He would give me advice.

> I don't know what to do without him. I feel like I'm trapped on my own and there's no escape. Everything is so serious and so heavy and it does get to be too much.
>
> The only time I feel happy, the only moments where I laugh, are when I call Rom. That's when I can switch off and take a break from the real world. That's when I feel normal again.
>
> I really depend on Rom a lot lately. He's someone I can release to, who I can confide in and say anything.
>
> But I really miss Kai. He was my person – and now he's not there. I need him.

I don't think many people in the world can say this, but in a weird way, Covid was a blessing of sorts for my family. In the first stretch of the pandemic, most BMX competitions were postponed or cancelled, plus travelling anywhere wasn't possible, so I was home. So too was my dad, who flies around a lot for work.

It meant that more people could be with Kai and the responsibility wasn't just left to Mum. BIRU had a one visitor at a time policy, so the three of us took turns every day to go in and keep him company, talk to him, lift his spirits, take lots of photos and videos of his moments of progress, and encourage him.

For me, and for my parents too, I suppose, the goal each day was to get to the end of it. By that, I mean that no matter what we were doing with Kai, whatever the task was, that we'd personally just take it moment by moment.

Slowly, little by little, he made progress. His days were filled with physical therapy, speech therapy, occupational therapy and much more. His first week of physical therapy was sitting himself up on a physio bed for two minutes, to rebuild his core muscles after months of immobility. It still makes me smile when I think back to the first time Kai swore at me. After spending all day in his wheelchair, the only real relief he found was lying flat. One afternoon, after we'd finished all of his therapies, he was trying to tell me something – but his words weren't making any sense. We both grew frustrated, until suddenly he yelled, 'I just want to go on the fucking bed!'

I got the message loud and clear.

> 7 APRIL 2020
> Helensburgh, Australia
>
> Spent the day with Kai. He did well today. He talked to me a little bit more than before. Although I don't understand what he is trying to say sometimes.
>
> He held himself up on a seat for five minutes. New personal best which the physio was happy about.
>
> I saw some more smiles from him too. So many positives. And I saw the Kai in him while he was doing his last exercise of the day.
>
> Pushing and leaning forward. I could see he was giving everything.

Although he couldn't speak, and was probably confused about whatever was going on, Kai was always going to give it everything. That was his way.

For all the life-changing damage done, while I watched Kai get stuck into the therapy, I saw something in Kai's eyes that told me that the accident hadn't robbed him of his values and beliefs. I knew Kai so well, so I was positive that right there, among all the traits that made my brother his unique and special self, was his constant determination to keep going. Those traits were still tucked away safely in his subconscious. Somewhere.

He listened to the experts. He did all the things that were asked of him, including the painful or tiring things he didn't want to do, from electromagnetic stimulation on his arm to endless sessions of speech and physical therapy.

We started a nightly ritual over dinner, something that we looked forward to every day. Whoever was with Kai for the day had to recount what happened, talk about what Kai achieved and show videos to prove it. These conversations around the dinner table between Mum, Dad and I were so uplifting. This way, we could see that Kai was making daily progress, whether big or small.

But at the same time, it was also a reminder of why he wasn't there with us at that dinner table, and the uncertainty that lay ahead for all of us.

Would Kai ever walk again?

Would he ever drive again?

STEP BY STEP

What would his long-term future look like?

These questions weren't asked aloud, but we could all feel them looming over us like a storm cloud.

I would often wonder what Kai was thinking and feeling through all of this. I mean, just think about it. Imagine the enormity of having to learn how to communicate again. Learning how to form words that are somehow both familiar and foreign at the same time, and how to organise them into a spoken sentence that's clear and understandable.

Think about having to master a movement you've done with ease since the age of two, but that your brain now can't remember how to do.

I still can't even imagine the level of frustration, anger and grief that must have come with knowing his legs used to squat 200 kilos, and now one leg hardly moved the way he was used to. Having to try for thirty minutes to open and close his right hand that used to grip onto a handlebar with ease. From being a super strong, professional athlete, to barely being able to move. It all would've been devastating.

There were so many times it felt brutal to watch. It felt so unfair. Almost cruel. I was angry at the world and impatient for my brother to be back. I wanted to fall apart so often.

But I watched Kai just get on with whatever the task was at hand. So I had no choice but to keep positive and support him the best I could. Every day was different, every day Kai achieved something new. And every day seemed brighter than the day before. It seemed like he was making exponential growth. And we were there right next to him, filming on our iPhones and giving him encouragement.

Kai's rehab schedule was full. Like, really full. Kai just showed so much enthusiasm to do everything he could. He didn't like sitting still, so we asked the therapists at BIRU to fill his day with as much activity as they could. Once the day of rehab was done, we would get on with some homework he was given. Whether it was extra physical exercises to strengthen his arm, or speech exercises. One of the exercises we did together often was a speech exercise. It was a 'finish the sentence' thing where there would be phrases like: 'A cup of . . .'; 'Fish and . . .'; 'Thread the . . .' and the challenge was to read the completed sentence. Everything was printed on a stack of A4 paper with pictures to give hints. It seemed pretty straightforward to us, but for Kai in the beginning, he struggled. He knew what he wanted to say but couldn't find the words. Sometimes he would blurt out a completely random, incorrect word with so much confidence that it would make me laugh. And then he would laugh too.

Through his rehab, I saw the old Kai, the driven, motivated guy. But I started to notice a side of him I hadn't often seen before – a side that didn't take life too seriously. He would laugh at himself when he made a mistake, and he really breathed life into the rehab rooms by making his therapists laugh. You could hear his laugh from a mile away. Through his driven mindset and positive attitude, he lifted the spirits of the patients around him, and pushed them to give it their best.

I'll never forget the day he stood up for the first time. It was on 30 April, during one of the physical therapy sessions. With the support of two therapists, he got on his own two feet. He let out a groan as he stood up as if his hips were tight from being in a seated position for so long. I swear my heart did a backflip. I was speechless for a moment and noticed just how tall he was. He towered over his therapists. Since he had been seated for the past three months, I had forgotten how tall he was. And his loss of muscle made him look even lengthier.

I filmed while some of the other therapists watched on.

'Wow Kai! How are you going up there?' one let out.

'Yay Kai!' another shouted.

And the whole physio room erupted in cheers and claps.

This was a big milestone. It was a glimmer of hope. A big one. Up until this moment, I wasn't sure how far he was going to get in his rehab. But watching him stand up was proof that if he could stand up, he could probably walk. If he could walk, he could do anything.

I think he felt it too.

I couldn't wait to get home and report to my parents the great news.

But like everyone, Kai had moments when he was quiet, and didn't have a smile on his face. I would ask what was wrong, but even he didn't completely know. As much as we wanted him to be happy all the time, the reality was that he was stuck in a hospital, alone for half the day, navigating a different body and doing rehab he didn't want to do. All the while I was out there doing exactly what he wished he was doing.

I did feel some guilt for continuing on training without him. But I knew it would be wrong if I stopped altogether.

In the wake of his accident, a feeling swirled in my head with a ferocity I'd never experienced before. For the first time in my life, I took ownership of my ambitions. I took my future into my own hands. All this time, Kai had told me when we would go to the gym, Kai would tell me what time the track session was and Kai organised the travel to different races. He was the coach, team manager and athlete all in one. I was one lucky sister.

Sure, I'd liked the idea of going to the Olympics before, but now I was obsessed with it. I didn't just hope I could win, I needed to, and I told myself that I had no other choice.

This determined new clarity was for Kai, not for me. He couldn't go to the Tokyo Games. He couldn't ever pursue his Olympic dream again. So, I had to. For both of us.

STEP BY STEP

I felt like I had a duty to carry on working towards our shared goal. There was a clear change in my thinking: I looked at my training schedule, I had regular chats with my coach, and I thought about how I could be a better athlete every day. There was a huge shift in the way I carried myself. I felt like I was beginning to be like Kai. I quite liked that feeling.

But could I even do it on my own? It was such a setback to lose my training partner. It was incredibly tough to chase the dream on my own without his support and encouragement. It wasn't meant to be this way. I wasn't supposed to have to battle solo, without anyone to lean on when it was exhausting or scary. No one to depend on. Whatever happened from this point forward was on me.

In May, Kai had a TV in his room at the BIRU, and sometimes he had the news on. I was there when it was announced that the 2020 Olympic Games in Tokyo had been postponed due to Covid.

'Did you see that?' I asked Kai. 'How crazy.'

'Yeah, crazy,' he replied.

But he was still in a haze. I wondered if he really understood what that meant. I wondered if he even knew where he was. I wondered if he understood what had happened to him.

I was kind of relieved when the Games were postponed. Since there was so much going on in my life, I could only imagine how my emotions might affect my racing. I was training hard, doing everything I could while following lockdown rules, but I could feel I wasn't in tiptop shape. Physically or mentally.

Having another year up my sleeve gave me the space to take a breath, focus on Kai for a little bit through the early months and then refocus. I saw the extra twelve months as an opportunity to get better and faster. I knew in 2021 I would be in much better shape than I was in 2020.

I knew I had to do everything I could to get fast. Which meant I spent some time in Brisbane training at the Olympic standard track at the Sleeman Sports Complex. I spent about a month or two there in the back end of 2020 through the start of 2021, then the plan was to do my last three months of final preparation for the Games there.

This meant I missed a lot of Kai's rehabilitation. By early 2021, he had graduated out of BIRU and into a transition facility before he would finally come home. He was in a good spot with his rehab. He was walking, talking and remembering things a lot more.

'We've got this, focus on your training,' my parents told me.

I trusted them, and I trusted Kai that he didn't need me. He had this and I needed to go chase our dream for both of us.

Time sped by. Before I knew it, the Tokyo Olympics were edging closer and closer.

STEP BY STEP

21 APRIL 2021
Brisbane, Australia

I can't sleep. My head is cloudy with so many thoughts about the Olympics. I've been asked a few times by media about what being able to compete at the Games would mean to me. Honestly, I don't know the answer. And that's been bugging me.

A small part of me doesn't want it to happen because it will require me to completely take control and ownership of my actions. I have to be the one with hands on the wheel. It's only me who can control how well I do. And I keep giving myself reasons to ease off and prepare for the fact that I might not win.

'I'm only young,' I tell myself. 'And I've been through a lot.'

It's tempting to give in to those excuses, but I know I'll be kicking myself if I don't keep myself accountable and maintain the pressure to go and get the result I want and know I deserve.

What does the Olympics mean to me? I don't freaking know. I can't even put it into words. What is my why? Why do I want to win? What does a gold medal mean? What am I doing this for?

I love improving myself every day and becoming a better athlete. I love seeing that progression in my training. I wouldn't give that up for anything. But why am I doing it?

Maybe it's Kai. He inspired me every day to be better and he was always someone who did everything better than me. Without trying to, he challenged me to be better and to push myself harder. He encouraged me to find more ways to get the best out of myself.

> His focus on winning made me want it too. He put me on edge and made me check myself, challenge my thinking and hone my determination. He made me feel guilty when I didn't put in the work and proud when I went the extra mile. He was my fire.
>
> I think I'm missing that crucial piece.
>
> My purpose was to be one half of this successful and extraordinary brother-sister duo who took on the world and won. My purpose was to continue to work as a team and make it. I wanted to go to the Olympics, but with him. I wanted it for him so much that I hadn't really considered how much I wanted it for me.
>
> And I was so sure that going to the Olympics together would be the start of our journey together. The beginning of a future. I wanted that. I wanted to share our dream. I wanted to make our dream a reality.
>
> My why has been taken away and I haven't figured out my new one. Maybe that's why it doesn't feel quite right. Like something is missing. I lost my teammate and my best friend. I worry it will never feel right.

I spoke to my psychologist, who I had been working with for about two years, about my missing why. She told me how she'd worked with plenty of athletes who were talented and wanted to win, but didn't necessarily have that really intense burning desire. The thing I used to have when Kai was part of the dream.

> **IT WAS A VIDEO OF HIM RIDING HIS BMX BIKE. I COULDN'T BELIEVE IT**

She reminded me that I have the ability and the skills to perform very well. I can win, and so maybe I don't need to have a why.

She said I could consider a purely execution-focused mindset. Be the best and win – that's the motivation. That's why I'm going. Maybe it's okay to have a gold medal as the goal that drives me, I thought.

A few months out from Tokyo, I had just finished a session of downhill sprint training when it started to rain and I had to call it quits. When I got back to the car, I checked my phone and there was a message from Kai.

It was a video of him riding his BMX bike.

What! I couldn't believe it. I knew he had been working hard to get back on his bike, but I had no idea he was so close to doing it. I don't know if I've ever seen a more joyous and uplifting video, and I watch a lot of reels, so that's saying something. I honestly didn't think he'd be able to do that again, and there he was, pedalling away, with ease might I add!

I was so surprised and very impressed. I watched it over and over again, a huge grin on my face.

He'd come so far in such a short span of time. He wasn't the same, and life was always going to be challenging for him, but he was determined to make the absolute best of it. He wasn't giving up. He wasn't slacking off.

STEP BY STEP

After all that had happened, he continued to inspire me. What an incredible guy, to be able to offer that. Such a legend.

Maybe he was my why after all. Kai. His dream. Our careers together.

I could do it for those reasons. It would be my burning passion.

CHAPTER FOUR
HARD HIT

The format of BMX racing at the Olympic Games is different to the World Championships or the World Cup. There are twenty-four men and twenty-four women who race, divided into groups of six.

On day one, these competitors race the same rivals three times, collecting points along the way. Then, the top sixteen men and women go through to the semi-finals, which happen on day two. That's another three races around the track – race, rest, race, rest, race again.

The final is held later that day to determine gold, silver and bronze medal winners.

BMX racing is a sprint sport that requires a huge amount of power.

In my view, when it comes to what it takes to win, the start is the most important part. If you're front of the pack by the bottom of the start hill, your chances of winning increase drastically.

That's what the hours spent in the gym are for. To build up your strength so that you can explode out the gate and get in front. Then you use your skills of jumping, manualling, pumping and cornering to maintain your speed around the track.

By the time I arrived in Tokyo, I felt so proud of myself, more than I ever felt before. I was proud of my preparation and how I had applied myself. I felt immensely proud of the change I saw within myself after I took responsibility for my training.

For the first time in my life, I felt like I'd given absolutely everything I had to reach a goal. I understood every phase of my training, I understood the purpose of each session, I set goals to achieve along the way. I even looked at my nutrition, recovery strategies and did a whole bunch of heat acclimatisation to prepare for the humid heat of a Japanese summer.

Yes, I'd trained for races before, but I had never put so much emphasis on the details. And I never wanted it so badly before. When I set foot in Tokyo, I felt the strongest I'd ever been, the fastest I'd ever been, and I was ready.

What I didn't account for was that I hadn't raced for about a year and a half. Covid largely put a stop to competitions in Australia and I didn't make it to the World Cups that were held months before, so I had absolutely no idea how I matched up against my competitors.

But I did the best I could.

During the practice days before qualifiers, I was fast. I could tell I was probably one of the faster riders there, which gave me a boost. I felt pretty confident.

29 JULY 2021
Tokyo, Japan

Finally, the day is here! I feel pretty freaking good. I slept really well and felt refreshed when I woke up. The weather looks nice too.

Today's task is clear. Race three laps. I'm confident I will make it through and execute the best possible performance.

I just need to go. Just fucking go!

The track in Tokyo was pretty long: over 450 metres. It equated to about an extra ten seconds of all-out sprinting compared to tracks that I am used to. Imagine telling a 400-metre runner they'd have to run another 100 metres. It's not something you can do if you're not prepared.

On day one, as the qualification race inched closer, I started to feel super nervous. I got into my own head and found myself hesitating. I was at the Olympic Games, for goodness' sake. The pressure was on, and I also felt out of my element in the racing itself. I hadn't raced in ages. It was like I had forgotten what my routine was, my self talk – everything. I felt all out of whack. The whole vibe was weird. There was no one in the grandstands, it was eerily quiet.

My first race was rocky. I didn't know what to do when I got stuck at the back of the pack. I panicked, tried to make an impossible pass and almost crashed. I got dead last.

I vividly remember speaking to my coach afterwards. Things weren't going as I'd hoped and I was going a bit crazy.

'Is this pointless? Is my Olympic dream over?'

He shook his head. I still had two more quarterfinals left. I just needed to get off the mental rollercoaster I was riding.

'Stop thinking,' he told me. 'Just go for it.'

In the second race, I had a great start but I made some mistakes on the second half of the track which trampled my speed. My legs were burning, and I registered just how long this track was, and how I was not prepared for it. *Just go, Saya!* I would silently shout at myself. That feeling of seeing the other women pass me on the final straight and not being able to catch up, right at the crucial moment, really sucked.

In the third race, I managed to find a way to preserve my energy and keep my legs working. I stayed out in front for the whole lap and finished first. I also had the fastest lap out of everyone, which was a huge confidence booster.

But I was exhausted.

Thump.

I flopped onto the cardboard bed as soon as I got back to the athletes' village. A mixture of heat, emotional and physical exhaustion left me absolutely depleted. But tomorrow was a new day and I was optimistic it was going to go well.

I didn't sleep well that night and woke up feeling crappy the next morning. It wasn't the best start to my final shot at Olympic glory.

I phoned my psychologist from the track.

'I'm freaking out a bit,' I told her. 'I'm tired, I don't feel confident. I just don't feel good about this.'

'You don't need to feel good to perform good,' she assured me.

She reminded me that I just needed to get out of my own way and ignore the negative lies my brain was telling me.

I knew I was fast because of that final lap on day one. I'd shown myself just how fast I was. My body knows what to do.

I could do it again. I could switch off the noise and just let my body do its thing. I had a shot.

Just go, I told myself. *Just go for it.*

The first of the three semi-final races was a bit ordinary. I was battling with a rider for first position, but I made a mistake on the third straight that made me lose all of my momentum. I couldn't do much but to desperately try to regain speed, finishing fourth.

The second race was much better, finishing first. Comfortably.

That felt way more like me, I thought as I crossed the finish line.

It lifted my spirits and gave me a strong feeling that I could actually do this. For the first time in the last two days, I felt a smile grow on my face.

If I nailed the third race, I was off to the finals to vie for a gold medal. An Olympic gold medal – a medal for Australia, for myself and for the years and years of hard work and sacrifice.

Then the third race upended my plans.

I was leading the pack in the final stretch, going over a jump, when a rider sitting right on my tail clipped my back wheel midair.

I felt myself lose balance. I could sense that I was going down. And then the world went black.

I woke up feeling my body being rocked from side to side. I was strapped to a stretcher with my head locked in a guard, preventing it from moving, as six staff members hurried me to the medical tent.

I was so confused at first. I didn't know where I was or what I had been doing. Clearly, I had hit my head.

It felt like I'd had a weird but incredible sleep. Unlike any slumber I've ever had.

Normally when you go to bed, you're in a familiar space, you doze off, you're in a light sleep, then a deep sleep, and gradually you come out of it. You dream. You wake up in the morning and you're where you ended the day eight hours earlier. It's predictable and routine.

Waking up from a concussion isn't like that at all.

People were huddled around me, yelling my name, a look of worry in their eyes, their faces tense.

I was confused. One moment I was dreaming and the next I was on a stretcher.

At first, I didn't feel much. Then I experienced an intense moment of panic as my brain started to register the pain from the crash. I only started to make sense of what had happened as I lay staring up at the sky, seeing the Olympic rings on flags in my peripheral.

Oh crap, I thought as I tried to sit up, then quickly realised I was strapped in, unable to move. The six men were talking among themselves in a worried tone. I couldn't make out exactly what they were saying. Were they speaking Japanese or English? I didn't know.

Oh no. This isn't good.

I peered down at my arms. They were pretty banged up and my jersey was torn.

That brief moment of peacefulness was over. My heart felt as though it was trying to break through my rib cage. I was dizzy and disoriented.

This is not how it ends, I said to myself. *I'm not going out like this. I can still go to the final – I reckon I might just have enough points.*

There was a flurry of activity as I was carried into the medical tent. Doctors checked me over. Staff from the Australian delegation peppered me with questions. I could sense their concern – unlike me, they must've seen on the screens how brutally I crashed.

'When can I get back out there?' I asked. 'I'm still in with a chance, right?'

I can't remember who it was. Someone with Team Australia – I'm not sure who. But they looked at me and delivered the absolutely crushing news.

'Oh, mate. You didn't make it. It's over.'

I needed a good result in the last race in order to qualify for the final. Crashing out meant I received the points of last place.

Being out of practice from racing, and being too mentally unfocused, had totally stuffed me.

Even if I'd had the points to qualify, I was in no proper

HARD HIT

THIS IS HOW IT ENDS. I'VE LET EVERYONE DOWN

condition to race. I probably wouldn't have been allowed to due to having a concussion. Someone would've stopped me.

I was absolutely devastated. I hadn't felt that way too many times in my life – completely distraught and wanting to find a deep, dark hole to crawl into.

This is how it ends, I thought. *I've let everyone down.*

There was so much build-up, so much media attention and hype. So many people were generously cheering me on at home and putting their faith in me.

Subconsciously, without even really realising it at the time, I had fully subscribed to that perfect Olympic fairytale that had been drafted by others. I realised those tales only exist in fiction. This was real life, and nothing like I had hoped.

Kai couldn't be here because of the cruel nature of life, plus crappy luck. We couldn't be doing this together, as an unofficial team, like we had been for so long. So, it was left up to me. I had to make it happen.

It was unfair. It felt like I had suffered an injustice of sorts, and I felt every ounce of that bitter disappointment while I lay in the medical tent.

After I got cleared by the medical team, I headed back towards the track.

I cried, but only briefly, because I had to do an interview with Channel Seven for their Olympics coverage.

'I feel like I've let everyone down,' I remember saying to the interviewer. The rest of it is a bit of a blur.

HARD HIT

A media appearance was the last thing I wanted to do. I was devastated. I was also dazed, like I was having an out-of-body experience, floating above myself, watching all of this insanity play out below.

But that's how it goes. I was a willing member of Team Australia, I had put myself on the world stage and asked everyone back at home to watch me and cheer for me. I had a responsibility to fulfil all the obligations that came with that enormous honour – even though things hadn't gone how I'd hoped.

I wandered around the BMX venue in a bit of a haze. The finals were run and the medals were won. The winners were all ecstatic. Cheering, hugging and celebrating. I watched from afar, but I wanted to be just about anywhere else but here. Because everything felt strangely unfamiliar – like I had just been plonked here for the first time. It didn't feel comfortable.

This place where I'd spent the past few days suddenly looked different. I was so confused by that sensation.

And I had a cracking headache to boot.

2 AUGUST 2021
Tokyo, Japan

When I reflect back to the racing I feel so frustrated and sad and gutted. I feel jealousy towards those who won a medal and I can't stop thinking about the 'what ifs'.

> I'm having a hard time accepting the result and what is fucked is that I know I can beat ALL of them on the podium.
>
> I was the fastest one there. Yes, there may have been a good battle but fuck, I should have been in that final.
>
> I try to remember exactly how I felt during racing, before my crash, but my memory seems to be one big blur.
>
> It makes me so mad thinking about what happened. I was fucking in front, minding my own business!
>
> I can't help but hold a small grudge that I was taken down. JUST WHY? It really boils me up inside that that's how it ended. It wasn't even my fault and I HATE that someone took that away from me.

The day after I crashed, still feeling totally out of it, I did a live cross to Channel Seven's breakfast show *Sunrise*. I could see on my end exactly what people watching at home were seeing.

My face in one box and a replay of my race next to it. Or rather, the crash – playing over and over again.

I hadn't seen it yet. I had only just lived it. I probably wasn't ready to relive it so soon, given how raw my emotions were.

It totally threw me and I lost my train of thought. I really struggled to find my words. I haven't watched the interview back, but I'm sure it was a mess.

Seeing the crash in slow motion was another abrupt shove back to reality. I had failed. It had really happened. My Olympic dream had collapsed spectacularly for everyone to see. I wished I could disappear – click my fingers and be magically transported away from there. To anywhere. Instead, I was on live television. Talk about a surreal experience.

'You spoke well,' said the media guy who set up the live cross.

That was hard to believe. I stumbled over my words, I couldn't think straight, I was exhausted and I had a headache.

I tried to present a pragmatic outlook. Displaying a seemingly healthy view of what had happened. I said it wasn't what I had hoped for, but I would get up and try again. I wasn't done. I was determined to come back from this. That sort of thing.

'There's a difference between pain and suffering,' I said in one of those interviews. 'I'm not suffering and this pain is only going to make me stronger.'

In the days after Tokyo, my Instagram DMs were full of amazing messages from people offering their support. The volume was insane.

They said they were proud of me and saw me as an inspiration. They weren't focused on my failure. They were happy that I'd gotten so far. I was really blown away by that outpouring of love.

I tried to remember that I was still the same person. Yes, I had crashed. Yes, it was unfair. And yes, my Olympic dream had been snatched away. But it didn't mean I was any less of a person.

JUST GO

The downside to seeing those incredible and kind messages on Instagram was scrolling through my feed to see plenty of content from Tokyo. Including my crash. There was even a slow-motion video of the exact moment I went down. Just as I thought I was making peace with it, anger reared its ugly head again.

At some point in those first few days, I shared a post on Instagram too:

5 AUGUST 2021

I'm frustrated and still finding it hard to accept what has happened.

One minute I'm winning my last semi-final and the next, I'm on the stretcher surrounded by a medical team.

It has been almost a week since then, but I can't help but still feel upset and unsatisfied. I'm not the type to dwell on bad outcomes etc. but this one hurts.

However, I'm proud of the way I performed on both days, and I feel as though I put everything I have out there on the line. The preparation leading into this race was exceptional and I feel as though it showed.

Although I hoped for a better outcome, I know that I did everything I could and executed my best. Which is the ultimate goal.

And wow, I am an Olympian. This has been a huge goal of mine to make it to the Olympics and I must remember that just getting there is a profound achievement in itself. I'm so humbled by this experience.

> I've learnt that it's important to never let a result of an outcome define me. And I know that with time, I will accept it and it will only be added fuel to the fire for the next goal.
>
> I'd like to say another thank you to everyone for your support. Like I said, I couldn't be more proud to be representing all of you.
>
> Currently I'm managing post-concussion symptoms and trying to stay away from staring at screens as much as possible.
>
> Your messages mean a lot to me and I will get back to reading them soon. Thank you again.

I stole the idea that 'results don't define me' from somewhere. I can't remember where, but that definitely wasn't some original nugget of inspiration that came to me in the depths of my despair.

Anyone watching me on television or eating up my social media probably would've believed me. There was no reason not to. And perhaps in the moment, I even believed it myself a little. Or maybe I desperately needed to believe it.

I was saying and writing things that I thought everyone needed to hear. I was playing a character that the BMX racing community, that Australia, wanted and deserved.

In hindsight, I suspect a major part of me desperately hoped that my public persona would rub off on me. If I smiled enough, if I was philosophical enough, it might catch on.

It didn't. Soon enough I realised that I wasn't really believing any of the things I was saying. I didn't believe in much of anything anymore.

I couldn't wrap my head around the fact that the Olympics didn't play out the way I had imagined. I thought I did everything right. I trained so hard. I gave it my everything, I *wanted* this more than anything. I had won so many times in my life without training this hard. So why didn't it happen?

It was a huge blow to my psyche.

The harder I tried to play the part convincingly, the more I tried to deceive myself, the worse I felt. Not because it wasn't working, but because it felt inauthentic.

I felt like a fraud and a fool.

555

CHAPTER FIVE

THE AFTER-MATH

I was gutted, but at the same time I was also really desperate to pick myself up and get back to racing.

I needed it. I had to start winning again so what happened at the Games didn't matter anymore. I didn't want it to define me. I had to show everyone how good I was.

The World Championships were being held in Papendal in the Netherlands, three weeks after the Olympics.

I set my sights on that. I just needed to win it. That would be epic, and would totally wash away the result in Tokyo.

But straight away, my body began to make it very clear that it wasn't ready. At all.

Imagine if you were to take a peach and put it inside a plastic lunch box. Then picture yourself shaking that lunch box up and down, around and around, for a few seconds. The peach inside is still intact, but it's bound to be pretty bruised and beaten up.

That's kind of what a concussion is. Your brain gets hit by a sudden jolt inside your skull.

The brain is soft, almost like jelly, and it's protected by fluid inside your head that helps cushion it from everyday bumps. But if it endures a strong enough impact, that movement can cause changes in the way your brain normally works, at least for a little while. The movement of the brain inside your skull can stretch and even damage brain cells, causing temporary changes in the way the brain

THE AFTERMATH

talks to the rest of your body. That's why concussions can affect things like memory, balance, coordination and even your mood.

And it's why concussions are considered a type of mild traumatic brain injury, even though there's nothing mild about the way they can make you feel.

Concussions don't always look the way people expect. You don't have to be knocked out, and you might not even have a visible injury like a bump or cut. Some people feel the effects immediately, while others don't notice symptoms until hours or even days later.

That's part of what makes concussions tricky. You might think you're fine at first, but then suddenly you're feeling dizzy, fatigued or just out of it.

After a concussion, people experience different symptoms depending on the severity of the impact and how their brain responds. One of the biggest mistakes people make is going about their business as usual, thinking they can just shake it off. But the truth is, your brain needs time to heal.

Unlike a sprained ankle or a broken bone, you can't see a concussion, which makes it easy to ignore. But pushing through it, by going back to work, playing sports too soon, or even spending too much time in front of screens can actually make things worse and slow down your recovery.

Most of the time, rest will do the trick. If you take it easy for a few days, then gradually return to normal as your symptoms ease, you'll often be fine.

While many people recover from a concussion within a couple of weeks, some take longer to heal. And in rare cases, people can develop post-concussion syndrome, where symptoms like headaches and dizziness last for months. Sometimes longer, without intervention.

This wasn't my first concussion. I'd had three or four before this one but my experience this time was intense. I was worried about turning my head too quickly. My brain felt like it was swollen in my skull.

It's quite hard to put into words. But put simply, I felt off. My head didn't feel right. I was a bit groggy, a little dazed, sometimes confused. That sort of sensation.

And the headaches. Constant headaches. Sometimes dull, sometimes pounding.

My neck was really sore. My head felt so heavy and my mind was foggy. I was really sensitive to sound and light. It was like having a head cold without the runny nose or sore throat. It was unlike anything I had experienced before.

The TV being on, cars driving by outside, tools clinking and clanking while I worked on my bike. It all felt so loud – like blaring noise shaking my brain inside my skull.

THE AFTERMATH

My heart rate would spike quite high while doing things that ordinarily weren't overly strenuous. I could feel it beating – throbbing – in my head.

Yes, I was desperate to go racing at Papendal and win at the World Championships. My desire to do it was ever more urgent, but every passing day made me feel more and more panicked, and less and less confident I'd be able to perform in a race.

Years earlier, I had what felt like a really bad concussion and it sucked for a bit, yet I was still back to racing two weeks later and felt pretty much fine by then. That was my experience, and so I had expected the same trajectory this time around.

But this time was different. I would wake up feeling like crap and be hit with an instant sense of disappointment. The symptoms hadn't gone away overnight. Even if I didn't train, even if I took it really easy, even if I simply tried to rest and recover, the symptoms would still be there the next day, as soon as I opened my eyes.

Some days, I couldn't get off the couch. My head would be pounding so badly that the only small relief I might get was from being almost totally horizontal. But I couldn't watch television or go on social media, or even really read a book, so time passed by painfully slowly.

The minutes felt like hours. It was just me, alone with my thoughts.

It was so hard to cope with. Time was ticking and I needed to feel good again so I could race. It was all I thought about.

I knew how I was meant to feel and this was just about the furthest thing from it.

I spoke to Team Australia's medical staff about how I was progressing and how worried I was feeling that the symptoms didn't seem to be easing. They agreed that it appeared I had a nasty concussion. But they still seemed to think it was pretty standard and to be expected. They told me to really rest up and I should be fine in another week or so.

That would push right up against Worlds, which meant I'd be going into racing without having done much training. I'd be very unprepared.

I felt so much pressure to win in order to redeem myself, so the thought of not being in the absolute best position possible was quite unnerving.

About ten days after the crash in Tokyo, I felt okay, so I went to the track and I tried to ride.

It was a beautiful day. My body felt fine. At fifty per cent speed, I could roll around, manual, jump, and ride like normal.

Maybe I'll be okay!

Reality trampled that thought almost immediately when I started to feel light-headed and dizzy. I hardly did anything strenuous but the visual processing of the speed and riding was too much. I stopped riding and on the way home in the car, I closed my eyes feeling absolutely exhausted, and I had a cracking headache. I regretted trying and I was devastated. I began to lose hope.

I was wasting the days away when I should have been preparing for redemption.

The more time that went by and the longer I went without feeling any better, the worse I felt about racing.

It wasn't just the horrid symptoms, but also the lack of confidence I would inevitably feel. I needed to be able to trust myself and my body when I was on the bike, and I just didn't think I'd be able to.

During a session with my psychologist, I tried really hard not to cry.

I told her everything that was on my mind, especially my concerns about my concussion and whether I would be ready to race.

I told her how it felt like no one understood me. I had been talking to doctors, had MRI scans that came back all clear, but that didn't give me the answers to explain how I was feeling.

She suggested the possibility that maybe I wasn't ready to compete.

She made me feel like it was okay to not be okay.

I still felt a lot of hesitation about letting the World Championships slip me by. It was my next big goal after the

Olympics. Since that was probably going to the dumps too, I could hardly fathom the fact that I would walk away from 2021 without winning a medal from either of them.

So much of me wanted to race. Not because I was looking forward to it – I wasn't, I felt so terrible and so scared – but because I badly needed a win. I had to get back on top so the Tokyo disaster could just be a blip on the radar. An anomaly that I could move on from and everyone else could forget about.

The stress of the whole will-I-or-won't-I turmoil inside my head made it really difficult to rest. In the end I had to make the inevitable decision. A few days out from Worlds, I called it. I told the organisers I wasn't racing. It was a bittersweet moment. A flood of relief, but also intense sadness that this desperate need for redemption would remain unfulfilled.

I tried to convince myself that even if I didn't make Worlds, I could still race in the future sometime soon. There were plenty of chances coming up. There was a World Cup event in a few months' time. I just had to put my health first and try to get back to normal as quickly as possible.

Race day was a real challenge. I went to watch and be supportive, to make it clear that I wasn't slinking off into the shadows, even if I couldn't compete. But the whole time I was just waiting for it to be over.

THE AFTERMATH

Watching all the women race made me feel uncomfortably jealous. I didn't want to think about any of it. So I tucked up my emotions from Tokyo, bundled them up in a box and taped it tightly shut. Then, I buried the box deep in my subconscious, so I didn't have to revisit it.

It hurt to be on the sidelines, watching someone become a world champion, when I didn't even get a chance to try. I hated seeing any medallist from the Games or the Worlds pop up on my Instagram feed. I didn't want to see any success stories.

The truth was I was bitter, I felt robbed, I was angry and I felt like none of them deserved their medals. But I knew there was nothing I could do about it.

After Worlds, Rom and I drove to the South of France. As much as I was deep in heartbreak, I loved where we lived during the racing season, in a town outside of Avignon. Where we were surrounded by old buildings and you could smell the crisp scent of the grapes ripening in the summertime. It was calming and I hoped a change of scenery would help me heal from my concussion. Rom also competed in Tokyo. He was performing well but finished sixth in the final. At Worlds, his mind wasn't in it and he didn't do so well. He wasn't particularly happy with his results. He wasn't talking about it, so I didn't either.

That was one of the great things about our relationship, that our conversations away from training and racing were hardly ever about BMX. Rom could leave what happened at training at

JUST GO

'I WAS BITTER, I FELT ROBBED, I WAS ANGRY'

the track and switch off. He could be a human being. And that made me want to be the same.

I think that's an important part of being an elite athlete that's often overlooked. The ability to switch off. To separate the sport from the rest of life. And not let the worries of training bleed into the importance of enjoying the day to day of this tough profession.

After Worlds in 2021, my concussion symptoms continued to drag on. All I wanted was to be healthy again so I could race, so I could win.

But every day I would wake to a feeling that something wasn't quite right. There was this pressure in my head and no one I saw seemed to have any answers about why I was still feeling this way three months on.

Those that had advice all suggested the same thing – rest, don't strain yourself, give it time. A few had nothing much to say. No one seemed overly worried that I was still experiencing these symptoms for such a long time. It was clear that I had post-concussion syndrome. It's experienced differently from person to person, but for me, it manifested in having constant pressure in my head, and extreme fatigue when I tried to train or do some sort of physical activity.

For some reason, concussion is an aspect of neurological health and medicine that hasn't received as much research focus as others.

JUST GO

When you've got post-concussion syndrome there's even less information. No matter where I turned, no matter which type of healthcare expert I sought support from, I was left without answers. I felt exhausted, angry, and totally alone.

> **7 SEPTEMBER 2021**
> Avignon, France
>
> Felt so tired when I woke up and I had a headache. Last night was bad and then this morning was just the same as three weeks ago. Felt like I'm back to square one again, which really does suck.
>
> I made the decision not to train today and I thought about whether I was lying to myself. Whether I'm just lazy or unmotivated.
>
> BUT I really am not fit to train. My body has been telling me to rest for the past couple of days and it's time I listened to it. There's no rush right now and getting my head to 100 per cent is the priority. So I was okay with my decision and after we got back from the track I lay in bed and watched Netflix all afternoon.

Ironically, the days that were the most frustrating were the ones in which I'd feel pretty good for no logical reason. Days when I'd trained, gone to the gym, spent a long time looking at screens. But nothing – no symptoms. Only to find myself feeling crap the next day, as if I'd taken three steps backwards. I'd then spend so much time trying to analyse what I had done differently that

THE AFTERMATH

morning to set myself up for a symptom-free day. I could never put my finger on it.

I think there was really no rhyme or reason. My brain's next moves couldn't be predicted. These symptoms did what they liked.

And all the while the next World Cup, in Turkey, was edging closer. My next chance of redemption. But it was clear that my head wasn't ready. I didn't go.

I worried that my time in the gym was aggravating the symptoms, but then, if I had a break from working out or went too easy on myself, I'd slip into a funk and worry I was falling behind.

Then, a few weeks after Turkey, there was another European Cup race. *Hopefully I'll be ready for this one*, I would optimistically think.

Then I wasn't ready. Again. It was a constant back and forth, a mental dance between hope and realism. I felt like I wasn't getting anywhere.

In October, I pulled the pin on the rest of the season and went back to Australia, to get some more support and hands-on treatment for my concussion. Trying to get help through online methods wasn't cutting it.

I chatted to doctors and I was then referred to a physio in Narrabeen, two-and-a-half hours away from Helensburgh, who finally gave me an answer. Her opinion was that these ongoing symptoms were actually caused by a neck injury. I had suffered a kind of whiplash during the crash in Tokyo that had never been identified or treated. The theory was that I didn't have issues with a concussion at all – merely that my neck was stuffed.

Apparently, a lot of people mistake whiplash symptoms for concussion symptoms. There's a fair bit of crossover, and usually both are experienced during head trauma. People just assume it's one and not the other.

> **29 OCTOBER 2021**
> Helensburgh, Australia
>
> After the gym, I went straight to a physio that I was referred to and spent two-and-a-half hours there. She suggested that every concussion had a whiplash component and I was most likely still suffering from that.
>
> She did some treatment, which was very painful but really released some of the tightness in my neck and shoulders. She focused on my jaw too. I almost cried. Wow. It was the most pain I've felt in ages. No wonder I still have symptoms.
>
> We then spent about thirty minutes on this machine that tests your neck strength. She found that some of my neck strength was lacking. This suggests that I've had this strength imbalance for a while, and with a sport like BMX, I really need my neck to be strong all over. At the moment, it's not strong, which could explain some of the pain issues I had with my neck before Tokyo and the crash.
>
> Using another machine, we also found that my vestibular function is unbalanced. The vestibular system is responsible for spatial orientation, balance and the coordination of eye movement. It's

THE AFTERMATH

> located in the inner ear and works alongside sight and bodily awareness to basically keep you upright and steady. If it's impacted by injury then symptoms like dizziness, nausea and imbalance can occur.
>
> She put me on a machine that requires you to stand as still as possible on a firm surface, and then on a foam one, with both eyes closed, and then both eyes open. The results for when my eyes were open came back normal. But when my eyes were closed, the data indicated something was off. It suggests that while using visual cues to stability is good, the function of my ears for balance is weak.
>
> The good thing is that both of these issues are treatable. I can continue with my training but the physio suggested I come back for treatment twice a week. This is because the machine to train neck strength is only available at this clinic. I can get away with doing resistance bands to try to improve things, but it's not very targeted. It's not the best way to address these types of concerns. She said if I committed to these for about six weeks – twelve visits in total – I should see a big difference.
>
> I think it's worth investing the time I have to fix this ongoing issue. I need it to be better next year. I need to not suffer through this anymore. Coming back feels like it's worth it. I'll regret not trying.

This was fantastic news. There was finally an answer, and a clearly defined treatment, to get things under control.

I could see the logic in her conclusion. I was having so many issues with my neck, shoulders and back, so untreated whiplash symptoms from my last concussion could be the cause for it all. As much as I hated having to drive so far to see this particular physio, I felt like this was the only option. No one had given me any answers or solutions until now. I had never been treated for whiplash before. This was the answer, and I felt it would put an end to my misery.

Driving to Narrabeen and back two times a week meant I was spending a lot of time in the car. Listening to podcasts was my go-to. I flicked on a podcast with an interview with David Goggins. He's a former Navy SEAL, ultra-endurance athlete and bestselling author known for his unbreakable mindset and extreme mental toughness.

As I drove along the highway going 110 kilometres per hour, I listened to his words with fascination. He's the kind of guy who pushes himself far beyond what most people think is possible, like running 100-kilometre races on bare and broken feet, setting world records for pull-ups and embracing suffering as a tool for growth. *How the hell can he endure so much pain?*

But he wasn't always like that.

He had a pretty tough upbringing and battled obesity through his childhood and adolescence. He struggled with self-doubt and failed countless times when trying to achieve his goals, before deciding to transform himself through relentless discipline and an unshakable work ethic.

THE AFTERMATH

His philosophy is simple but brutal – most people quit at a fraction of their true potential, and the only way to find out what you're really capable of is to suffer, struggle, and keep pushing long after your mind tells you to stop.

I read his book *Can't Hurt Me* after Kai recommended it to me a few years ago. His story is incredibly inspiring. And in that time of suffering I was in, listening to the podcast reminded me that I need to pick up that book and read it again.

In the interview, the thing that grabbed me was hearing Goggins speak a lot about taking the hardest path, the one where nothing is handed to you. It caught my attention immediately, given I had just spent weeks trapped inside my own head, feeling beaten down.

There's something powerful about choosing the hard road, he believes.

It's easy to make excuses, but Goggins advises against easy exits. He is all about stepping into the fire, embracing the grind and proving to yourself, every single day, that you can take on more than you thought you could.

Hearing him talk about this idea of callousing the mind in the same way you callous your hands through hard work really resonated with me too.

My mind had been raw, exposed and vulnerable. Along with my concussion symptoms, I had let doubt and fear dictate how I felt about myself. After the disappointment of Tokyo and the crash, that voice in my head told me I'd failed. And the worst part? I listened to it.

And that's the thing about taking the hardest path. It sucks. It's uncomfortable. It pushes you to places you never thought you'd go. But when you come out the other side, when you realise you're still standing, still fighting and still improving, there's nothing more rewarding than that.

Goggins doesn't sugarcoat it. He says this path isn't for everyone. Most people will take the easy way out. Most will choose comfort over challenge. But if you really want to find out what you're made of, if you really want to smash your limits and surge beyond them, you have to be willing to suffer. To embrace the grind. To step up every single day, no matter how hard it gets.

And that meant I needed to start carving my own path forward while everyone else took the highway.

I felt like such a loser for feeling sorry for myself for so long. I realised my mental game was weak for letting one race derail me like this. *I shouldn't be feeling sorry for myself like this. How pathetic am I? I've got a solution to my concussion, I'll get better, I'll train harder and I will come back stronger.* I felt frustrated for using so much of my energy being angry at the past. Goggins was dealt a way worse set of cards than I was, and he still powers through any challenge in his way. In fact, he goes out of his way to challenge himself. I decided I was going to stop being the victim.

THE AFTERMATH

I had to stop blaming that rider that took me out at the Olympics. I should've been faster so she couldn't catch up. It was just as much my fault as it was hers. I needed to let go, stop letting the past define me. I was angry I'd let it control my life for this long. It wasn't her fault that I was suffering. I was choosing to suffer. That was the true difference between pain and suffering. Pain is inevitable, but suffering is a choice. Now I could make the choice to accept the pain and take control of my own life.

One morning, my friend Jaz took me out for coffee. She could sense that I was flat and made the sudden suggestion that we go for a bushwalk. I wasn't keen. But reluctantly, I agreed, and we jumped in the car.

We drove to the Wodi Wodi Walking Track in Stanwell Park. It's named after the local Indigenous custodians of the Illawarra region and it was only a fifteen-minute drive from my place.

Along the way, there are these glimpses of Aboriginal drawings and the remnants of ancient middens. Parts of the trail are challenging, with steep inclines and rough terrain. But it was a good type of challenging. And it was well worth it.

At the top, the scenery is spectacular. The view of the sprawling, crystal-blue coastline and back towards the lush and never-ending green landscape stopped me in my tracks. The air was crisp and clean, fresh against my face.

For a moment, I forgot about Kai's accident. I forgot about Tokyo. I forgot about my concussion symptoms.

I sat down on a rock, legs stretched out in front of me, my calves aching in a really satisfying way, and drank in the peace and serenity. I took a deep breath and let the salty air fill my lungs.

It was almost like the painful thoughts of the last few years were just too heavy to have carried up there with me. They'd stayed behind, giving me a brief reprieve. For the first time in a long while, my mind was quiet. It was a nice feeling.

There had been too much overthinking, too much stress, too much negativity rolling through my head for so long. But at that moment, it was calm. Nothing mattered. It was just me, Jaz and the view. The world and my life suddenly felt so uncomplicated.

After a long moment of silence, I heard her say: 'You're going to be fine.'

Perhaps it was a fleeting comment to shut me up, since I'd been complaining for the whole trek. But those five simple words held a lot of weight for me. It was a reminder that it's not that bad. So what, you missed out on one Olympics? So what, you couldn't race at the World Championships? It's not the end of the world. It was almost like a nudge to get out of my own head and think positively for once. Not everything has to be so heavy and serious.

THE AFTERMATH

And even though the experience hadn't given me any new answers, even though I was still in the exact same place I had been before we started climbing, I felt a bit different.

I felt as though I could believe her assurance – that I was going to be fine – in a way I mightn't have before. Someone believed in me. Someone had my back. I felt like it might take me a while to get there, that there was still so much work to do, but I thought that maybe I really would be okay.

I would get to the other side of this struggle.

CHAPTER SIX

SEED OF DOUBT

After the horror of the Games in Tokyo, and the disappointment of missing the World Championships, then the entire rest of the season, I turned all my focus to 2022.

It was January of 2022. I had finished three months of treatment with the physio in Narrabeen. Although training my neck and doing weighted repetitions on that machine was awful, I found pleasure in the fact that I was training; I was fixing myself. And I wasn't waiting around for the symptoms to go away. I found comfort in the fact that my concussion was healed and the only thing to do was to make my neck stronger.

It was a confidence boost to know that there was nothing wrong with me. I was okay. I was healthy and could go back to pushing myself in training without being overly cautious. I was so relieved to be back to this position where I wasn't thinking about how my head feels for weeks.

It was like a huge weight had been lifted off my shoulders. I could finally take a breath and focus on getting faster.

The months that followed the Games weren't enjoyable, but now I had high hopes for the year ahead. I felt eager to get back to racing. Not just eager, I was desperate. I couldn't relax until I'd competed again.

I was working on a new plan. To get super fast, incredibly fast, so I would always be front of the pack and no one could crash me out again.

SEED OF DOUBT

It sounded good on paper – train my way out of trouble. But on my first race back, everything went wrong.

It was 14 January 2022, and I was in West Palm Beach in Florida in the United States, there to compete in the first round of the American national series.

I wasn't feeling overly hyped about racing again. I felt nervous, and I felt I'd placed a lot of pressure on myself to do well. I *needed* to do well. But all I wanted was for it to be over. I wanted to just get it done.

I noticed that I had developed a fear of hitting my head. It had taken months to get symptom free, and I didn't want to go through that again. Each time I got on my bike I felt a bit scared.

On race day, the venue was filling up with spectators and riders. The rock music was pumping through the speakers getting everyone hyped up. On the other hand, I found it hard to focus. On the gate, trying to listen to the gate call, I would be distracted by the commentators over the PA system talking. Everything felt off.

But I made it through the qualifying rounds and into the final.

One more lap. Just go, I thought, giving myself a pep talk.

In the final, I had such a good gate start and I felt strong. I was out in front, in line with two women who were either side of me – I was sandwiched between the two, all of us fighting for the top spot. As we got closer to the first corner, things got tight. The rider on the outside of me was coming in hot – too hot. I stopped pedalling to back off. But she kept coming and took out my handlebars.

There was no time to react and, in a flash, I was on the ground. The girl on the other side of me also got caught in the crash. I was badly winded. Crushed by a wave of pain all over my body. For so long, I struggled to breathe. I couldn't get words out without needing to take big gulps of air. It felt like I couldn't get enough oxygen into my lungs.

As I got my breath back and the paramedics helped me to my feet, I saw two overlapping circles in my vision. Like a dotted Venn diagram obscuring my view of the world.

At first, I thought I was just feeling a little dizzy from standing up too fast. But no matter how many times I blinked or breathed in deep, those circles in my vision didn't budge.

You've got to be kidding me, I thought. *Not again.*

---

14 JANUARY 2022
West Palm Beach, USA

They were thin, but I had circles in my vision that looked like TV static.
In-between and surrounding the circles, my vision was clear, but that was weird too.

SEED OF DOUBT

> It seemed like my brain couldn't process what I was seeing in that particular area. Meaning I hit my head.
>
> Fuck.

I got checked out in the first aid tent and they urged me to go to hospital. I wasn't sure it was worth it. What could they do? No one last year was able to help. And besides, the pain everywhere else was my primary focus. I was in tears, my ribs hurt so much. I just wanted to get out of there.

When we got back to the Airbnb that Rom and I were staying in, I thought I'd be able to tough it out and get through the night despite the pain, but when I tried to lie down it wasn't good.

I began to worry that maybe my injury was worse than I thought it was. I needed to know if I was okay, because I didn't feel it. I burst into tears and sobbed.

I really didn't want to go to the hospital, but I asked Rom to take me. We got there late, around 9:30 pm, and there was hardly anyone there.

The fewer people, the quicker I can get out of here, I thought.

Then they told me Rom couldn't stay with me due to hospital Covid policies, so I found myself there alone. It was dark outside, and the hospital gave me an eerie feeling. It was deadly quiet except for the shuffling of nurses going back and forth.

Finally I saw a doctor. They gave me a CT scan on my head and chest to rule out major head trauma or a collapsed lung, and other scary injuries like that.

They found bruising on my lungs, which explained why my ribs hurt and breathing felt difficult. My head was fine, but they agreed I probably had a concussion. Again.

I went back to the Airbnb exhausted, but glad I had answers. I was going to be fine. No major injuries, I'd just be in pain for a bit. *I'll keep showing up*, I thought. *Tomorrow will be better.*

The next day I made it my mission to avoid my phone and really focus on concussion recovery. That meant a dark room, a podcast and eating nutritious foods to help fight the inflammation in my brain and body.

It meant closing my eyes and resting in bed all day.

I was relieved to find I didn't feel a headache when I woke up the next day. I was being quite cautious about my head, but I felt fine.

A few days later, I joined Rom at the BMX track. The weather was nice, sunny but not too hot. I was comfortable in a t-shirt and shorts. But any movement kept reminding me that I was hurt. I could do some things in the gym, but I couldn't ride yet.

I was so angry to be here again – injured, unable to ride, feeling sorry for myself. This crash took a massive chunk out of my confidence and sense of self. And it planted a seed of doubt.

SEED OF DOUBT

> I'D DEVELOPED A FEAR OF RACING

This was not supposed to be the plan. I was supposed to be training to get faster than my competitors, yet it was clear that what I'd done for preparation wasn't enough because that girl on the outside was faster. That was why I crashed. If I had been faster, none of this would've happened.

But now I was stuck here recovering, while my competitors were training and getting faster. I felt like I was falling behind for every minute that went by. And I felt that the more unprepared I was for the next race, my chance of crashing would only increase.

When my head wasn't throbbing and my emotions weren't boiling over, I tried to reflect on what happened in the lead-up to the crash that afternoon in West Palm Beach. What stood out was how scared I felt.

Throughout the whole event, I kept catching myself just wanting to leave.

Get this race over and done with, I'd tell myself in frustration. *This is so hard and so scary and I need it to be over.*

I knew that wasn't the right mindset to be in. That's the worst possible way to go into anything.

But the outcome simply meant more evidence that racing equals crash, and crash equals hit head.

I'd developed a fear of racing. I had literally started to fear for my life when I got on my bike, ready to race. My brain told me that when I did, I was going to get tangled with someone, crash and get really hurt. There was no other conclusion to be drawn.

SEED OF DOUBT

How do you compete like that? What kind of state is that to be in, and be in constantly?

The fact that I crashed on my first real race after Tokyo just made it worse. To me, it was clear evidence that I couldn't get through a single event without getting hurt.

Is this what it's going to be like? I asked myself. *Is it just the norm now that every time I race, I crash?*

In February that year, Rom and I flew to Houston in Texas for another race. As the plane landed, a wave of anxiety crashed into me. It was so severe and the message it brought with it was clear. I didn't want to race.

Suddenly, I was terrified. My fear was choking me.

Maybe I'm just not cut out for this, I thought. *Will I ever recover?*

---

2 MARCH 2022
Houston, USA

Everything is fucked. I'm fucking so stressed now. I've never felt like this before.

Holding back tears, I tried to calm down. Track warm up. I hated it. Fuck, honestly, I HATED IT. I was trying to smile and talk to people but all I could think of was how much I didn't want to be here. Because being here meant that I had to race . . .

I really couldn't do it. This was more than just anxiety. Anxiety I can control. I can manage negative thoughts but this was different. This

> was KNOWING that I'm not ready for this. This was knowing that I don't have the evidence to back up my positive thinking. And this was knowing that I'm not willing to put myself in this position where it's a possibility I can get hurt and take another step backwards.
>
> Am I being scared? Am I just trying to avoid an uncomfortable feeling? I don't think so. The thought of getting on the gate with seven other riders just fucking stressed me out. I'm not willing to do that.

I decided to pull out of the race. I really couldn't believe in myself. I felt like I had inadequate training, and by putting myself in the race, I would get hurt.

What did I think? That I'd just magically get my confidence back? That I could just get on a track and feel like the old Saya again? No way. I barely recognised her. I was so far from that confident person that I almost forgot what it had felt like to be her.

I kept trying to focus on the fact that life is hard, that some things we experience are difficult, and all of that is natural and to be expected. This sport is challenging. There's a reason the stakes are so high and the field is so competitive. Not everyone can do it.

I had to accept that getting myself back to form was going to be a challenge and require a major adjustment. Did I think it was impossible? No. Did I think I could do it? I thought so.

Soon, there was a small glimmer of hope. After Houston, we went to Rock Hill, South Carolina for another race two weeks

SEED OF DOUBT

after. The track was less daunting, more forgiving if I made mistakes. And I had almost two weeks to train on the track to get my confidence up. As much as I felt the nerves and anxiety, I felt like I had evidence that I was going to be okay. I knew the track and I knew what to do. I felt like I could race.

That weekend, I felt that confidence. And I showed myself that I was fast. One of the days, the wind was howling. In hindsight it wasn't completely safe to race, but I went out and raced in spite of it, and despite the fear I felt.

I found myself stepping up on the podium having placed second. I was so happy. I was so proud of myself. It showed me that I am physically good enough. I'm fast enough. It's just my fear that's holding me back. If I could just find a way to shut off this fear . . .

I needed help.

It was nowhere to be found.

CHAPTER SEVEN

THE SPIRAL

As the 2022 season continued, fear became a monster in my head.

The fear centre of the brain, the amygdala, is a little almond-shaped pocket of nuclei that controls the big emotions. It's a key part of the brain's limbic system, which takes care of emotions and behaviour.

When the amygdala spots danger of some kind, it triggers the fight-or-flight response. It wants the body to act, and act fast, whether that's to run away from the situation or stay to fight. Fear is the most potent motivation. But to be effective, the amygdala has a whole filing case full of vivid memories with very clear emotions attached to them. When it detects fear, that drawer is flung open and a specially curated recollection is retrieved and thrust into your subconscious.

No matter how many pep talks I gave myself, I found myself hating life at races more and more. I thought I should feel more confident. And yet I felt unprepared for every race I went to.

There were so many moments where I would've given just about anything to be pretty much anywhere else. But I would try to catch myself in those moments. I'd try to snap out of it, reminding myself that nothing in life is enjoyable one hundred per cent of the time.

The tough times are what make the great times worth it. You can't have one without the other. That's life – everyone's life.

THE SPIRAL

But it was becoming an almost daily battle. I felt like I wasn't progressing in my training, which would lead to loss of confidence. All the while the next race would inch closer and closer – a race I felt wholly unprepared for.

I'd try to rally my inner thoughts to be more on my side. I'd tell myself I was capable and strong. I was worthy of trust. But it felt like an uphill battle.

I had to stop looking at racing so negatively. It was toxic. My thoughts just kept cycling back to this now deeply held belief – this fear – that I was bound to crash. But I just couldn't help it.

At one European race in Verona, Italy, I tried to look at BMX as this purely neutral thing – not good right now, but not bad either. Just something I do and a part of my life. The track was demanding, high speed with big jumps. Every part of me wasn't enjoying it, because of the fear I felt. So I tried to divorce it from negativity and accept that challenges would come and go. Racing is just a testing day – an opportunity to learn and grow. I told myself to think of it like an experiment to try taking the pressure off myself.

Let's just go and see what happens, let's try that and see if the result changes, I'd say to myself.

I didn't have to be beside myself with enjoyment through all of it. It could be an almost academic exercise. An opportunity to reveal more about myself and my progress. That race weekend

I finished fourth on day one, then eighth on day two, when I slid out in the corner trying to make a move in the final.

Despite the fact that from the outside it looked like I was doing fine, inside I was so uncomfortable. Even in practice sessions, the negative voices in my head were so loud, I was surprised no one else heard them.

If I rocked up to practice before the race and there was a breath of wind – not enough to push me off my bike but enough for me to notice it – it would make me doubt myself more. In these conditions, when it is windy but not extremely so, the way to get through it safely is to jump as if there is no wind. As soon as you jump with hesitation, or stiffen up in the air, that's when it becomes dangerous.

You have to jump with commitment, conviction and confidence. Be at the front of your bike, which is an aggressive position, instead of at the back, which is defensive. The more you can commit and trust yourself, the safer you will be.

Intellectually, I knew all this. But mentally and emotionally, the wind frightened me. And what if I couldn't trust myself to jump even without wind? I was freaking out.

Why does everyone around me have smiles on their faces?
Isn't this scary for them?
Why does it seem like I'm the only one?
Oh, that's right, it's because it is hard for me. I've had it tough, I would think.

Maybe I had unresolved feelings about Kai's accident. Maybe being scared was just who I was now.

Others are so lucky not to be like me, I'd think.

I'd been totally consumed by that ridiculous sense of urgency. It meant I couldn't just go with the flow. It meant I forgot how to trust myself and my body.

I was so focused on winning straight away, when I should have been focused on getting experience, regaining my confidence and learning from the entire process. I'd thrown myself in the deep end, entering almost every race I could and expecting to come out of it stronger and more confident.

It wasn't working. In fact, it was making me less and less confident. I had to stop rushing. I knew I would benefit from taking a step back, starting small and working my way up. Taking the time to work on building confidence, one step at a time. But I was already in season, Australia had paid for me to compete, and I couldn't just back out now. I felt like I had no choice but to get on with it.

But nothing is more dangerous than when doubt is backed up by evidence.

I had achieved so much. But I stopped seeing myself as capable, as strong, and as someone who could do hard things. Instead, I saw myself as someone who might fail. And when that happened, when I started thinking like that, I stopped giving myself the chance to succeed.

JUST GO

Some days, I lost. Some days, I listened to that voice and I pulled back. I played it safe. I told myself that I was just being smart – I was avoiding a crash, an injury, a failure or a disappointment. But deep down, I knew the truth. I knew that it was me who let the voice win.

---

16 APRIL 2022
Zolder, Belgium

Today's race was the European Cup in Zolder in Belgium. And it really sucked. It was a hard day and I felt mentally drained from the get-go. I felt like I didn't come into today with a solid plan and an objective. I had this unresolved question going through my head about what I wanted to achieve here. Did I want to win or just do my best? I couldn't decide.

In the final, I'm not sure what went through my head. I had a good start. A great start! I nailed the first jump and saw that I was basically in second place. There was some heat from the rest of the pack and things were getting tight in the corner. I instantly backed off, let everyone in, and gave up basically. It was over.

It was so crappy. I was so upset with myself that I didn't try. That's the main thing that hurt – I didn't want to put myself in any danger, I didn't want to accept even the tiniest risk to myself, and it meant not defending my line and not being aggressive to fight for positions.

Watching myself come dead last really sucked. I know I can do better and I'm sick of not trusting myself. I'm sick of being in this state,

THE SPIRAL

of not being in control of my own riding. I'm letting other factors determine what I can do and dictate my approach. In reality, I know I have the skills to put myself in uncomfortable situations and make it through to the other side.

I hate that I can't trust myself. I hate how different I feel. Where did the old Saya go? What happened to her? I miss her so much.

I have to stop thinking that the world is out to get me. I'm looking at racing through such a negative light. I'm not even enjoying it anymore. All I'm doing is 'trying to survive' when I'm out there. I'm so obsessively focused on avoiding a crash. It's as though I've decided that's all I'm capable of. Crashing out. I know that's not true!

I'm better than this. I'm more than capable of being aggressive and racing hard. So, why can't I?

It's so easy to fall into the trap of continuing to feel sorry for myself. It means there's no pressure. All of this is totally out of control, and so I don't need to achieve anything. But nothing is going to magically make these challenges disappear. These struggles won't be overcome by not taking some accountability for my role in them sticking around.

I need to be the one to make them go away. The only chance I have of beating them is by actually DOING something. Putting pressure on myself. Actually trying. I need to stop being passive and make it happen. I need to step up. I need to realise that I am fast enough, I can be safe, and I can win.

JUST GO

I spoke to my psychologist about these feelings. She told me that these races could help me to rebuild my confidence and hone my skills, but only if I let them. In order to beat this fear, I needed to get back out there and keep putting myself in these uncomfortable situations.

She suggested I have two or three objectives for each race weekend. Not broad and results-reliant ones like 'win'. But an objective like, 'Challenge my negative thoughts'. Or, 'Commit to fighting the urge to hesitate.'

It would place some responsibility on me to build up my sense of worth and to recognise my capabilities, she suggested. That would help with my confidence.

It was all much easier said than done.

There weren't many times throughout the 2022 season that I felt truly confident. I felt dissatisfied with everything I was doing. It was such a struggle and the number of days I was having where my mood was really low began to worry me.

When I tried to think about why that might be, the list of possible reasons was pretty long.

Plus, BMX didn't give me nearly as much joy as it used to.

> 19 MAY 2022
> Avignon, France
>
> I feel like every single day I have thoughts of quitting. I'm beginning to gain perspective and understand that maybe BMX isn't who

THE SPIRAL

I am. Not entirely. I'm beginning to understand the concept of 'results don't define me as a person', which I've said to myself before in the past, obviously, but without really getting the meaning of it.

At this point in my career, I don't even like BMX as much as I used to. Or, in honesty, I don't even know if I ever loved it. I can't be sure. Have I truly continued because I love it or because I don't want to quit?

Did I continue because Kai did, and I couldn't picture myself being anywhere else but by his side while he pursued his dream? Our dream.

Through the wins, the travelling, the lifestyle, the fame, the popularity, all of the fun stuff that has come to me as a BMX racer . . . Is it really worth it? It feels like my health is on the line. My life feels like it's suffering. At some point, I think I have to make a decision about whether it's all worth it. I feel like that time is coming. Really soon.

I'm in such a difficult place. The challenges are too big. If I make a decision right now, at this moment, feeling how I feel, will it be biased? Will I make a truly objective choice with so much clouding my thinking?

Maybe I should stick it out until Paris. It would be crazy not to, right? It's in a little over two years, which isn't that long in the grand scheme of things. I think I really want to experience another Olympics. I think I need a different experience to the one in Tokyo — one that's on my terms and not determined by crappy luck that's entirely out of my control.

JUST GO

Even if I don't win a medal, being a two-time Olympian counts for something. Right? That's a good goal to aspire to. To be at another Games would be so awesome. I want it. Not for the status. Not for anyone else. Just for me.

Maybe I just want to be a champion. Worlds or Olympics. Anything. I want to be able to call myself a champion and to be the one that beats everyone else. The best in the world. Even if it's just for a brief moment. I want that.

So, it leaves me in a difficult position. I want to be a champion but then what I want isn't completely in my control. It's difficult to know whether I'll ever get there. Even the goal of getting to another Olympics, of making it to Paris. It's possible, but anything can happen. I might not make it, and then what?

I guess I can only attempt. I can only do the best I can, and if it doesn't happen, hopefully I'll be content with my other achievements. Hopefully I will have grown as an athlete, and a person, and can celebrate a more resilient mindset and a sharper determination after all of this. Maybe I can face and overcome my fear. Maybe I'll realise that fear is a sign of being on the right track and that I'm chasing something great and worthwhile.

Maybe I can get to a place where I'll be really, truly happy, even if the results don't show. I've always thought I had to be the greatest BMX rider ever, but maybe being remembered for my willingness to not give up, to push through heartbreak and fear, and to improve myself, is worthwhile. Those would be nice things to be known for. Those are champion qualities, I think.

I think it's pretty clear that I want to continue. I know I'm not in the best state of mind right now. But maybe if I start to focus on

THE SPIRAL

> the things I do love – being challenged, setting goals and achieving them, the places I get to go and the people I get to meet – then I can shift my thinking. Perhaps the best plan moving forward is to just try to enjoy the things about BMX, about my life, that I like.

This was the mental state I was in. Exhausted from the conflicting emotions, and feeling like I was holding onto my BMX career by a thread.

In June 2022, I found myself racing a World Cup in Papendal, Netherlands. During practice for the race, I was feeling incredibly hesitant on track. I was rigid on the bike. Nervous.

It's normal to experience nerves on race day. To feel your heart race or your hands shake. It's a totally natural response to a challenge. Those physical sensations only have an impact on the way you perform if you let it. But I had completely subscribed to the fear, so now I saw those sensations as warning signs. I took them as indications that I shouldn't be doing this and that I was the only one feeling this way. It made me doubt everything.

That's no state to be in when you're racing at an elite level and trying to win. And from a purely human perspective, quite literally fearing for your life when doing your job is a really messed up thing to experience. It's draining.

On race day, I felt strange. I felt out of place, I couldn't focus. My mind was racing with possible scenarios that hadn't happened yet. But I got myself up on that start hill and lined up for my first race. At the gate waiting to go, I was trembling with fear. I was absolutely terrified, but I knew I couldn't back out. Backing out wouldn't help anything. I needed to push myself.

Just go.

The gate went down and I was leading!

Wow really? Great. Let's go!

Then a girl took a tight line around the first corner and passed me on the inside. I decided to fight back for the position instead of giving in. I fully committed to make the pass on her inside. Then it happened again. She came over to reclaim her position, my handlebars got caught on her torso and I was on the ground. Knocked out cold. That familiar blackness came rushing towards me, yet again.

One major concussion on its own is bad. Multiple is serious.

---

17 JUNE 2022
Avignon, France

Well, shit. It's a full week after my crash and I'm lost.

I had another concussion. Another one. I can't believe it. It's not good at all. After everything I've been through, after all the hopes I've pinned on this year and what I need to achieve, this is what I get? Another crash and another hit to my head?

Yesterday was a bad day. I cried a lot. I just kept wondering how long this is all going to go on for. I was feeling heavy concussion

THE SPIRAL

symptoms straight away and I dreaded what that meant. Would they stick around for a few days? A few weeks? Or longer? I hate to admit it, but I know the answer. This many big hits in such a short amount of time means a quick recovery is just not going to happen.

I asked myself so many questions that I didn't have any answers to. Ones that only stressed me out to think about. Ones that made me feel like all BMX is bringing me is negativity and pain and heartache. Is it worth it anymore? Do the positives outweigh the negatives? It's so upsetting to think about because I think the answer might be no.

Last night, when I couldn't stop crying, I almost began screaming at myself. Stop crying you freaking loser! What are you doing? You're so pathetic! I was so mad at myself. I hate feeling like this — being like this. I went from being absolutely beside myself and in tears to feeling furious. Like, grow up. Your life isn't that hard. So many people have it way worse.

I took some deep breaths and tried to steady my mind. Eventually I was able to fall asleep.

I haven't thought about training for the past few days. I wake up and I have nothing planned. I watch Netflix. I'm lazy. And honestly, it feels pretty satisfying. It's almost a relief.

But then today, I noticed just how horribly grazed my knuckles are. It triggered me so bad. It was a reminder that I crashed and that I was knocked out. It felt so embarrassing. Like, seriously, another one, Concussion Girl? Congratulations. I feel like such an idiot. And pathetic. How the hell does this keep happening? Why can't I learn from the previous ones and stop getting hurt?

JUST GO

Maybe I should change helmets. Maybe that's something I should've looked into ages ago. Am I dumb for not doing that already?

I put a post on social media about fear, being kind of vulnerable about feeling fearful lately. It had only been up for a few minutes and I suddenly felt sick. It took every scrap of self-control within me to not delete it. Am I dumb for being too open? Am I dumb for thinking I can be the best at this sport when clearly I can't even stay on a bike? Am I dumb for trying?

Why do I keep hitting my head? I'll take anything but a concussion! I hate it. I hate that I'm the girl with all the concussions. That must be what people think of me, right?

I don't know. I have no idea what's going on inside of my brain. In my soul. Something seems to be holding me back. I can feel it. Maybe it's something that I haven't addressed.

These past few days, I've imagined what it might've felt like if I hadn't crashed and I had won or at least made the podium. When I picture it, I don't feel stoked. I think it would've been surprising and pretty amazing, but I don't think it would've felt deserved. To be honest, I don't think it was mine for the taking. If I hadn't crashed and I had won, I reckon it would've been luck.

I'm training, but I don't know if I'm entirely putting in the work. I'm just not progressing. I'm not seeing clear improvements. I don't feel satisfied with what I've been able to achieve. I think it's because I'm holding back. Something is holding me back. Those aren't qualities that should exist in a podium rider. That is not the behaviour of a winner.

THE SPIRAL

A really crappy part of that particular crash was that I couldn't escape it. Not just the pain, not just the symptoms, and not just the feeling of terror – but seeing multiple high-resolution photographs of my head hitting the dirt.

The day after, Rom told me one of the event photographers had posted a sequence of images of the impact. It made me instantly want to vomit. I started to sob uncontrollably.

It was not okay. I wasn't okay! Concussions were not okay and me having one – another one – was not something to be proudly shared and shown off to the world by someone who happened to snap some really clear pictures of it happening.

I felt broken. After knowing those photos were circulating, I spiralled. I hated the way I was feeling. I hated the person I saw in the mirror most days. I hated the fact that I'd had so many concussions.

I didn't cause the crash entirely on my own. But I was the only one that crashed. Why did I go for that move? Was it too risky? Was my fear of crashing, of hitting my head and getting hurt, putting me in a dangerous mindset? Was I leaving myself vulnerable by being too on edge and too hyperaware?

Was I responsible in some way for all the terrible things that had happened? Could I have prevented some or all of them from happening? Maybe if I wasn't so scared. Maybe if I was on top of my mental fitness.

"I WASN'T OKAY! I FELT BROKEN"

THE SPIRAL

All I had done was take all of the pain, disappointment and anger of what happened in Tokyo and tried to turn it into motivation. Raw fury converted into motivation. If I could just win the next race, if I could take out the season, then what happened in Tokyo wouldn't matter. Everyone would forget how I failed. I would forget that my Olympic dream had been shattered in such a spectacular way. I would feel valuable again.

I rushed.

I thought I was doing what I needed to do. I thought I was approaching the season exactly how all elite athletes would. But I'd thrown myself into it at the expense of my health and wellbeing.

I was so desperate for redemption that I never gave myself a break. I never decompressed after Tokyo. I never allowed myself to start from scratch and rebuild. I went straight from the horrors of Kai's accident and the long-lasting and intense trauma of the time that followed – which was also unresolved in so many ways – into preparing for the Games. No break, no time to stop and check how I was doing.

A week after the crash in Papendal, I returned to our base in the South of France. I took a break from training, accepting that this recovery wouldn't be quick or easy. Summer was starting to settle in, bringing the kind of dry, blistering heat the South is known for. The cicadas had begun their relentless chorus – sharp, rhythmic, and almost deafening in the countryside where we live. I remember lying on the couch, the sound echoing in my head, merging with the ache in my body and the weight of reality sinking in.

I was sad a lot. And I got really sick of feeling so down. Then I would feel even sadder about being sad. It was this vicious cycle that never seemed to end.

I couldn't be okay or satisfied if something wasn't absolutely perfect, and there wasn't much that fit the bill. Instead, I just felt petrified that I was being left further and further behind.

But another feeling was becoming stronger too. I questioned what I was doing.

I wondered what the point of it all was. Was it time to leave BMX behind for good?

I quickly set that thought aside. There was no time to be thinking too deeply about my future in the sport. Nor was now the right time to even think about this. I needed to focus on my recovery.

The World Championships were set for six weeks after Papendal. This all seemed too familiar. Crashing, hitting my head, not being able to race Worlds.

Will I be ready? Will six weeks be enough? I thought about the last time I was in this position, only eleven months ago, and how long it took for me to recover. And get confident racing again – which still hadn't happened.

THE SPIRAL

After days of going back and forth with myself, trying to make a decision, I finally realised I needed to let go. I had to accept that I wasn't going to race at Worlds.

> 30 JUNE 2022
> Fuschl, Austria
>
> I need my brain to live. I need my brain to have a family and have a long life.
>
> I don't need a 2022 world champ title to live! So let's fuck it off. It's gone. It's done. No Worlds for me. It's simple. I knew it. I knew it from the start. And I KNEW that it's not going to be enough time but I let other people tell me something different when I knew it really wasn't realistic.
>
> This is my brain! Fucking hell. Why am I treating it as though it's my wrist that is broken. It's my brain. It needs to be treated properly. Whatever it takes. I need my brain to be functioning and 100% healthy in order to live. And that's going to take time. And that time would be well invested if it means I lower my chance of having to deal with concussion shit later, and honestly my life is WAY more important than the World champs.
>
> I will find the strategies to cope with what happens that week. I will be okay and I will survive not racing.

CHAPTER EIGHT

A GLIMMER OF HOPE

A week after my crash in Papendal, I had the opportunity to go to Red Bull's Athlete Performance Center in Austria. I got so much support there, from physiotherapy to specialist advice. I had a team around me that cared, monitored my symptoms and wanted to get what was bothering me sorted.

They knew what I was feeling, both in terms of the symptoms of my concussion as well as the frustration at the lack of answers. I didn't feel quite so alone. Sometimes that is all you need to make it feel a little better.

A week later, Red Bull then arranged for me to travel to Switzerland to a specialised concussion treatment centre. It's a dedicated facility that's favoured by lots of high-performance athletes who've had brain injuries. Ice hockey players, football players, motocross racers, you name it. When I got there, I saw signed photos of elite athletes with messages thanking the team at the centre. It gave me hope that if these professionals helped them, they could help me. I knew I was at the right place.

In an intensive two days of testing, they tested every facet of my brain function. Balance, speech, memory, cognitive ability, eye movement – the whole lot. I did all kinds of exercises so my responses could be measured. I had MRIs, CAT scans and ultrasounds on various parts of my body.

They were so thorough. It was intense, a little overwhelming at times, and pretty exhausting, but I also felt this strange sense of excitement. For the first time, I felt like I was being taken seriously. I felt heard. And the careful attention being paid to me gave me some desperately needed hope.

There were a few things that showed up on the test results. One of the biggest findings had to do with my eye movement. In a nutshell, rather than my eyes moving smoothly from right to left, they moved in an uneven, juddering motion.

I had a condition called ocular motor dysfunction. This is where the eyes have trouble moving, focusing or working together properly. It affects how well the eyes track objects, shift focus between distances or stay steady on a target.

They also found that I was experiencing visually induced dizziness, a type of vertigo triggered by complex visual environments. It happens when the brain struggles to process a large amount of visual motion or conflicting sensory information. People with this condition often feel unsteady, light-headed or off-balance in situations where there's a lot of visual stimulation, like in a busy shopping centre, travelling in a fast car or even just watching fast-moving scenes in a movie.

Normally, the brain takes in information from the eyes, inner ear (which helps with balance) and body in order to figure out where you are in a space. But if your brain is relying too much on your vision and gets overwhelmed, say, by a crowded street with lots of movement, or scenery whizzing by as you travel in a car, it can cause dizziness and discomfort.

And finally, because of those two conditions, I was also suffering from cervical dysfunction – problems with the muscles, joints or nerves in the neck that cause pain and stiffness.

When the cervical spine, which is the neck, isn't moving or functioning properly, it can lead to tension, inflammation and nerve irritation. This can create a domino effect, impacting everything from head and shoulder mobility to how the brain processes coordination and balance.

This is also congruent with whiplash symptoms, which sounded familiar from my experience at the physio in Narrabeen just a year ago.

When the doctor explained to me the kind of impact these dysfunctions can have on someone, I could've burst into tears. She was outlining the exact symptoms I had been feeling for so long. It felt like I finally had an answer. A clear answer.

The best news was that these conditions could be treated with therapy, which involved different exercises, like eye tracking exercises or balance exercises. I was overjoyed.

What's incredible about the brain is that when one area is lacking after a head knock, other parts take over to try to pick up the slack.

That's great for a while, but the longer those areas of the brain are working overtime to compensate, the more strain that's endured. It's an inefficient way to function. And there

A GLIMMER OF HOPE

> "I FINALLY HAD AN ANSWER. A CLEAR ANSWER"

are consequences. So, I needed to retrain those areas separately until they were back to working the way they should.

Everyone I met with at the concussion centre felt confident that we could treat and beat these three challenges. They were really invested in making me feel like myself again. And they explained everything in a way that I could understand.

They gave me a two-week program, told me what time to come into the centre for treatment, and after each session, they would give me homework to do.

After they pinpointed the things that needed to be focused on, I had a surge of determination that I hadn't felt in a while.

It was an incredible feeling to finally have answers about what was wrong with me. At long last, there was clarity and, more importantly, a foundation on which to build a plan of attack.

---

12 JULY 2022
Winterthur, Switzerland

I'm in a good headspace. I'm putting myself as the priority now. Not training. Not even thinking about BMX. It's really nice and not seeing it on social media is so great.

I'm having little check-ins throughout the day to work on myself, asking, 'Am I doing the things I want to do for myself?'

For some reason I started doing some research on the internet about concussions. I knew this already, but one site mentioned something about the increased risk of dementia after multiple concussions. I'd

> be lying if I said I wasn't worried. Fuck. I've had a lot of concussions and it's really not good. It raises questions in my mind about whether it's worth continuing.
>
> I am so devastated to be put in this position. I can't forget the fact that this is a fucking risk. Is it really worth it? What will I be saying to myself if I have another one?
>
> These are hard fucking questions and they scare me so much. It really is a drastic change to what I thought my next few years were going to be
>
> But I don't want to give up. I don't want to stop like this. I really want to go through these steps. I want to better myself and I want to enjoy riding my bike again. Racing could be another thing I decide later!
>
> So I decided I won't be racing for the rest of this year. I'm not ready. Yes, it feels like a long break but in the grand scheme of things I think it will be fine.

During my stay in Switzerland the Noëths, a BMX family who knew my dad, opened their doors for me. I was so grateful. I was alone in a foreign country with no support while I went through some intense rehab. I didn't want to be there, going into hospital a few times a week, treating a concussion. But being with a kind of foster family made the whole situation not so bad.

Even though I had answers to my lingering questions about concussion, the number of concussions I'd had was weighing heavily on my shoulders. What about my long-term health?

I'd given up on racing Worlds, I'd given up on racing the rest of the season. Should I just give up altogether?

What if I crash again and hit my head? This is the best place to get treatment and I can feel myself getting better, but I never want to have to come to this centre again. I tried my best to stop these trains of thought, and convinced myself now wasn't the time to think about this.

At the end of my stay in Switzerland, they ran a whole new round of tests – the ones they'd done when I arrived. The results were really impressive. My eye movement was back to normal. My balance was fixed. My symptoms – dizziness, headaches – had gone away. It was incredible. There was not a single doubt in my mind that my concussion was healed. Physically I was back to normal, and my brain function was probably the best it had been for some time now.

The centre was absolutely top notch. They took such good care of me. I was really grateful.

Now, reflecting on that experience, I can say with absolute conviction that it changed my life.

I felt like a new person, in so many ways. I was happy – relieved, even. But that joy was short-lived, shadowed almost instantly by a heavy, unshakable question: what now? Could I make a comeback to BMX, or was I chasing a future that no longer existed?

CHAPTER NINE

AT A CROSS-ROADS

I'd never felt so lost and empty before in my life.

Six weeks after the Papendal World Cup, I went to watch and support Rom at the 2022 World Championships in Nantes, France. I watched on, seeing the riders race off the eight-metre start hill, jump the ten-metre jump at the bottom all while being so close to one another.

I felt zero envy. I was happy to be on the sidelines; I knew I wasn't ready for it. I couldn't think of anything worse than being a part of it.

I started to wonder if I was even cut out for this sport in the first place.

How can all of these girls do it so fearlessly?

How did I do this before?

What happened to me?

As I sat in the grandstands watching the racing, the crowds erupting with cheers of support for the riders, I felt like I was in my own world. Not living in the present but inside my own head. I was confident that my symptoms had faded away and I was completely healed from my concussion thanks to my time at the Swiss Concussion Centre. Now, I spent a lot of time battling my own thoughts, facing life-changing questions about how and if I was going to continue racing BMX.

My fear of racing had grown and mutated into this unimaginably huge monster inside of me. It felt uncontrollable,

AT A CROSSROADS

unbeatable, unavoidable. Eventually, after wearing me down every single day, I felt like it destroyed me.

After the World Championships I went back to Australia. I continued to train and ride at local BMX tracks around my home, but I heard myself tell people openly that I was feeling scared about racing.

I was saying those kinds of things to myself, too. Not just other people. And I was saying them a lot.

In the past, I was able to manage these thoughts. I could acknowledge that I was anxious or scared, and then I could counter it with evidence and belief – that my chances of crashing were low, that I had the skills to avoid hurting myself – to overcome the fear and do it anyway. I wanted to conquer the challenge more than I wanted to give up.

But now, after having two concussions back-to-back, I felt like I was in completely different circumstances. I was really worried about the risk of crashing again and hitting my head. I've seen first hand how brain injuries can manifest and I was terrified of what it might mean to have so many concussions. I had very little belief left. Racing this year while I wasn't ready had beaten me down even further.

I thought that putting myself in challenging situations, like throwing myself in the deep end, would help me rebuild my confidence, but it really hadn't.

> **MY FEAR OF RACING HAD GROWN AND MUTATED INTO THIS UNIMAGINABLY HUGE MONSTER**

AT A CROSSROADS

The thought of racing again scared me. I could feel myself tense up and hesitate just by thinking about it.

I realised that I hadn't completely confronted the devastation, resentment and bitterness about what went down at the Games. At the start of 2022, I felt like I had overcome some of it, but still those memories surged back, dragging with them emotions I thought I had buried.

The thoughts about giving it up came more frequently. I thought about how much less stress I'd feel if I did.

> 27 JULY 2022
> Helensburgh, Australia
>
> I went out to dinner alone. While I was sitting there, I watched someone get this incredible-looking alcoholic drink. Some kind of cocktail. I sat there and thought about how nice it would be to just have a few of those and not think about the consequences. Normal people stuff.
>
> Imagine what my life might be like if I was 'normal' and wasn't constantly thinking about training, racing, gym, keeping to a strict routine, working to a rigid schedule, and all the rest of it. Would I still be happy? Would I enjoy life with the absence of BMX?
>
> Hell yeah. I reckon I would. It would be so much less stressful, for one. And for two, I'd have so much flexibility. And way, way less risk of serious injury. Another big plus.

> I could do whatever I want. I could eat and drink whatever, whenever. Mostly. I could stay up late and sleep in. I could skip the gym. I could book a holiday at any time of the year, without having to consult a schedule of global races to avoid even the slightest chance of a clash.
>
> I could never get on a bike again if I wanted to.
>
> It's crazy how much sacrifice is needed to be an athlete. So much that has to be missed. An awesome concert the week before a meet? A friend's wedding on the same day as a World Cup race? Not possible.
>
> And that's not to mention dealing with injury and feeling constant pressure to perform — to be the best, every single time.
>
> When I get to that inevitable point, will I have any regrets? Will I wish it had ended sooner so there was time for more? More . . . anything? Everything?

This year, I was supposed to get confident. I was supposed to rebuild myself and reflect and learn. I was meant to embrace the discomfort and put myself into as many different situations as possible so I could improve. But it was so hard to stay focused on that goal when it felt like I was on a totally different level.

I should be on the podium, I'd think to myself, resentful and jealous.

But should I? There wasn't much evidence to show that was true.

AT A CROSSROADS

By the second half of 2022, I'd see others racing the rest of the World Cup season, held in Bogotá, Colombia, that I'd decided not to race at, while I was back home in Australia. I'd scroll through social media and see their training updates, their podium photos, their wins stacking up while I was struggling to imagine myself racing again.

And it wasn't just the results. It was how effortless they made it look. Their confidence, their momentum, the way they seemed to be gliding forward while I was stuck in place.

It wasn't even jealousy, not in the way people usually talk about it. It was something worse. It was this deep, sinking feeling that I'd lost something I might never get back.

I had raised my hands in defeat, waved the white flag, and welcomed the fear in. Once it won once, it only got stronger. The next time, it was so much harder to fight back.

Watching the competition unfold in Bogotá, I didn't wish that I was racing at all. All I felt was bitterness towards the sport. And towards myself too.

That was confirmation to me. I couldn't do it anymore. I was exhausted. I couldn't spend a huge chunk of my life being terrified. I couldn't stagger through with these terrible symptoms. I couldn't continue to be a lesser person than I should be and deserved to be. I didn't want to wind up seriously injured and I didn't want to die.

JUST GO

> **24 SEPTEMBER 2022**
> Helensburgh, Australia
>
> I told Mum I'm thinking about quitting BMX. We'd gone for a walk and suddenly it felt like the right time to talk to her about it. And we did talk — a lot. She told me how she'd thought more than once lately about telling me to quit. After my last concussion, the thought was stronger than ever in her mind.
>
> I'm glad she didn't. I'm glad that I was able to get to this point on my own and not wonder if I'd been gently guided here. Or pushed.
>
> She was so supportive. She encouraged me to listen to my heart and make the right decision for me. And she told me that if I quit, it doesn't mean I'm done succeeding and winning in life. I can do anything, she told me. I have so much left to give. Who knows where I could go next? I'm young. I have a whole world of opportunity still to explore.
>
> Most of all, it suddenly felt like I wasn't alone in this. For so long, I'd been walking around with this heavy burden — this tightly guarded secret. I worried about what people would think if I spoke it out loud. I worried about disappointing people, about them feeling like I'd wasted their time by walking away now.
>
> Mum made me feel seen and heard. It felt so good to tell someone.

When I thought about it after our walk on that cool afternoon in spring, BMX had caused me, Kai and our parents so much pain.

AT A CROSSROADS

I can't fathom how horrifying it was for my parents to almost lose their son, and then to spend every day for weeks and weeks watching him cling to life. The long and painful months that followed as Kai learnt how to talk, walk and move again. The setbacks, the challenges, the enormous energy and effort required to progress – it was so hard on him, but also on my mum and dad.

If I crashed and was seriously injured, I'd feel so guilty about my parents having to go through that again. I would feel so selfish that I pushed on with something that had already cost me so much in terms of my health and wellbeing.

One of the major reasons I was so heavily invested in this sport and in this goal of Olympic glory was because of Kai. It was his dream that became our dream. If he wasn't with me, what was I doing this for?

It was my life. It was my brain. I had to live with the consequences of the decisions that followed – not anyone else, and especially not those influencing my way of thinking.

Honestly, my life was about way more than BMX. Or at least it should be. If I wound up with some permanent, life-altering injury from this sport, what would the next few decades look like? What would the rest of my time on this planet look like?

Damn it, I thought. *I should've just fallen back on my tried and tested method of making decisions from the start of this whole nightmare: What will I regret not doing more?*

JUST GO

Taking proper care of my brain was the easy answer, obviously. It was a no-brainer. No pun intended.

I was going to quit BMX.

10
10
10

CHAPTER TEN

NOT DONE YET

I was at peace at last. Deciding to quit BMX racing felt like a heavy weight had been lifted from my shoulders. My health was no longer at risk. But then, on a cloudy afternoon in October of 2022, my psychologist offered a suggestion that made me feel sick.

'Have you thought about watching back some videos of Tokyo?'

I definitely hadn't. Not once – not one little bit. I couldn't think of anything worse. Why would I want to relive one of the most crushing experiences of my life?

I had refused to watch any footage from the Games – whether it was practice or racing. Videos of me winning and the video of the crash. I even avoided photographs from the Games because any reminder of how it all unfolded was too painful.

My psychologist felt like I had spent too long running away from the pain. Not only had I failed to process the gravity of the moment, but I had forbidden myself from feeling any of the emotions attached to it. The abrupt loss of a dream. The dashing of the biggest hopes. The sadness. The rage.

'You've got to feel all of that,' she said. 'Find someone to watch it with and then experience it. Feel all of those emotions.'

Maybe if I confronted it, if I fully felt it in its entirety, and talked about it, I could finally let it go. I could mourn and move on. Even if I didn't see a future in BMX, I could put it to rest finally, at long last.

'I think you need to stop avoiding it. It's time to face it, Saya. Appreciate where you got to as a big achievement. Realise the good that surrounds it, let go of the bad.'

On the morning I decided to do it, I asked Mum if she had some time that afternoon to sit with me while I watched. Even asking her the question brought up emotions, and I was already fighting back tears.

I knew this was going to be uncomfortable.

We sat in the living room side by side as I opened my laptop.

All the footage from the Games was there, ready to go. Starting from the embarrassing first race of the quarterfinals, we watched them one by one.

7 October 2022
Helensburgh, Australia

I really didn't want to watch the footage, but it felt like time to confront what had happened and see if there was something — anything — to be learnt from it.

It was exhausting. The mere decision to watch it was emotionally heavy in itself and I wanted to cry before we'd even hit play. It only got heavier from there.

I cried a lot. Especially watching the crash. I had to force myself to keep watching, to keep my eyes open and focused on the screen. It was important not to look away and to take it all in after so long.

JUST GO

Watching my rounds before the crash was just as hard. It was so clear that I hadn't done that well. In actual fact, there really were only one or two laps that were good. One or two out of five. And my third straights on virtually every race were slow. I was running out of gas and everyone was catching up to me.

After watching the videos, through heavy tears, verbalising my inner thoughts to Mum, I came up with a few conclusions.

I was fast. I was quick out of the gate and was a really strong contender, for a while at least, but my second half was really slow. No wonder they caught up.

Everyone else was fast. Bethany, Mariana and Merel were all really, really fast. And they deserved their medals. Contrary to what I thought in the past.

Something unfair happened to me. It was really unfortunate that it happened at the Olympic Games, of all places. But it happened and there's nothing I can do about it now.

Now, with this information, I can either let it keep affecting my life or I can let go of the 'what ifs' and move on.

I want to close this chapter of my life and stop allowing it to take emotional energy from me. It was so unfortunate but shit happens to good people — that is just one of those things.

I worked my ass off. I considered every little detail. I devoted myself entirely and without question to getting a gold medal. I did it all to an extent that I never have before. For that to amount to nothing, to not get the result I so desperately wanted, was devastating. I

> think it left a permanent bruise on my soul. It's more frustrating than anything I've ever experienced in my life.
>
> This is a lot to take on. These are bittersweet realisations. How ironic to have this kind of closure right at the point of walking away from BMX. That was my one and only shot of going to the Olympics, my sole chance of bringing home a gold medal. That breaks my heart.

I had avoided confronting what happened in Tokyo for so long. It was this terrible, painful thing that had happened, and I naively believed I could move on from it by ignoring it. Pretending it never actually happened to me. By throwing myself back into racing.

The only thing I let myself think about was how bitterly unfair it was. How wronged I was. How I absolutely would've won, without question, if not for that stupid crash.

I had avoided any visual reminder of the entire Olympics for so long. In the end, that decision just caused me more pain. And by avoiding the reality of it, I never accepted that maybe I wasn't robbed of anything.

Just because I wanted to come home with a gold medal so bad, I'd worked so hard for it, and I'd earned a shot at it, doesn't mean it was my destiny or something. I realised that's not how the world works.

The stark reality was that I fell short. I trained hard. I gave it my all, but I wasn't consistent, I didn't have enough endurance to get around the track and I wasn't the best racer there. It was heartbreaking but it was the truth. I had to accept that I wasn't good enough. Keeping up the delusion was only going to prolong the pain.

It was a turning point, watching the Tokyo race back. It brought a clarity I so desperately needed, and it allowed me to draw a line in the sand.

And it planted a seed – the idea that I had some unfinished business to attend to.

Around this time, I'd had this sudden idea of what I might do with my life if I was to walk away from BMX. It came out of the blue, totally unprompted, in a way that took me by surprise.

I should try track cycling.

BMX racing had given me a strong foundation. Explosiveness, bike control and speed – all of that translates well into track cycling. In fact, there's a lot of crossover between the two sports, especially in the sprint events. Some top-level track cyclists started out in BMX racing. The skill set transfers well – particularly the power and intensity required in short, tactical races.

But what drew me to the sport wasn't just the familiarity. It was also what it didn't have.

Track cycling doesn't have many of the environmental variables that make BMX so dangerous. It's raced indoors, meaning no wind, no rain, no weather-related safety risks. There

"IT WAS HEART-BREAKING BUT IT WAS THE TRUTH"

are no jumps. Just smooth, fast, focused racing on a steeply banked wooden track.

That difference mattered to me. After years of pushing limits in BMX, I had started to see the risks differently. I was no longer willing to accept the dangers that had once felt like part of the thrill. I still wanted to win – but I wanted to do it in a way that allowed me to train and race with focus, not fear.

Track sprinting appealed to that mindset. It's a purer test of physical power, speed and strategy. It's about how much force you can put through the pedals, how quickly you can accelerate, how well you can out-think your opponent. It's about raw performance.

Yes, crashes still happen. Top-level sprinters can hit speeds of sixty kilometres per hour. In events like the Keirin – where six riders jostle for position behind a pacing motorbike before launching into an all-out sprint – collisions can be severe. Riders get tangled up. They go down hard. I've seen it. It's brutal.

But even with that risk, I saw track cycling as a safer and more sustainable path than BMX. The environment is controlled. The equipment is optimised. The focus is on strength, not survival.

I knew the transition wouldn't be easy. The bikes are different. The riding position, the gear ratios, the techniques – they all take time to learn. And the tactical side of sprint racing is complex. Timing and decision-making are just as important as physical strength. But I believed in my ability to adapt. With the right mindset, I knew I could do it.

Track cycling represented a new challenge. A clean slate. A new way to chase greatness – with fewer risks, and no excuses.

One day, I had the opportunity to join the track sprint team of the NSW Institute of Sport (NSWIS) for their training session. The session was held at Dunc Gray Velodrome, the only indoor velodrome in New South Wales.

I remember it being dark and a little rundown. The smell of the wooden boards reminded me of the old gymnasium at my Japanese primary school.

As I jumped onto the matte black Dolan bike the coach gave me, I considered what could be my new daily training environment. The bike was a little too small for me and the atmosphere was gloomy, to be honest. But at least I would be safe.

That was the main thing. No weather to consider, no one to make me crash for now. I could just get strong and be fast.

I knew it would be different, but I quickly realised that there would be a lot to learn. I tried not to dwell on that too much.

It was a steep learning curve. I had to be more over the front of the bike than I ever had before. I needed to be in an aero position, then bend my elbows and position myself lower towards the bike than I was used to.

It was really hard. It was difficult to pedal in that position and I felt like I was putting in my absolute best but not getting the speed I thought I should. That made me feel like I wasn't trying hard enough, even though I was giving it my all. Make that make sense!

I trained with the NSWIS crew for a few weeks. The athletes were nice, but I could see how much I had to learn and train. My legs would burn in just the warm up, so my endurance would have to be significantly better.

The thing with BMX racing is that we don't pedal all that much. We pedal hard down the hill, then get in a few pedals as we come out of a corner, and sometimes we sneak in a couple of pedals between jumps. The rest of the lap, we keep our pedals in a completely static position – instead we gain speed by bending our knees and manipulating the body to manoeuvre over jumps. Clearly, my legs weren't built to pedal so much for so long. In contrast, the track bikes have what is called a fixed wheel, meaning that the pedals turn if the back wheel is turning. In other words, you can't stop pedalling on a track cycling bike. You can't keep your pedals in a static position and 'coast'. Your legs keep turning as long as the bike is moving forward.

Despite the challenges, it felt good to be doing something after such a low period. It felt good to be challenging myself with something new. Something I'd be less likely to hurt myself with.

But that feeling didn't last.

One training session with NSWIS, the team were talking among themselves about the Track World Championships that were happening that week.

Oh, I should definitely watch that, I thought. This was my new sport so I should scope out what it's all about. Maybe eye off my future competition.

When I got home from training, I flopped on the couch and tuned into the livestream of the racing.

16 OCTOBER 2022
Helensburgh, Australia

I just watched the Track World Championships. I saw two exceptional French riders — a young girl who got gold for the 500-metre time trial and another who won the women's match sprint.

Watching it brought up a whole heap of yucky emotions. I always feel anxious or nervous thinking about track and whether I really have a shot. So many doubts in my head about whether I'd ever really make it. Those girls are younger than me and already way, way ahead. Am I stupid for thinking I could win a rainbow jersey?

I feel this immense sense of pressure, this need to rush. I feel like I'm running out of time and I'm starting from a position that's so far behind where I should be. I mean, I am. This is a whole different game and there are only going to be more and more girls coming up that are fast. Faster, probably. And they're going to get faster. My head tells me I'll never be able to catch up.

JUST GO

> Am I willing to try this even if it means I never win? If I know now that there's a strong chance I won't win, that I won't reach the same level of success I have in BMX, do I still want to do it? What am I doing it for? Is it to fill a void within my self-worth?
>
> I'm putting my sense of self-worth in things I can't control. Is that what I perceive as success? Social media followers? Am I being ambitious or seeking validation?
>
> I'm so unclear. I want to be clear.
>
> I don't know where I am. I have no sense of direction and when looking for my purpose, for the thing that guides me and grounds me, all I see is fog. I feel like I'm always sad and unsatisfied lately. I'm wondering what it means to be happy. This is so unlike me.
>
> Even though I'm young, I feel like I don't have the luxury of time. The more I think about it, the more I fear I'm making the wrong decision with quitting BMX and trying track. Even in those moments when it seems so logical in my head, there's a dull squeeze of my heart that implies a jolt of doubt. Or is it a warning? A warning from my soul?
>
> Am I making a good decision for my future or am I simply running away from pain? From the source of my pain – BMX, or rather the past few years of BMX. Is it really no longer serving me well, is it really the right time to move on and begin writing a new chapter, or am I just giving up so I don't have to feel scared anymore?

It's a really confronting thing to make your mind up about something major – or at least to believe you have – and then suddenly question the decision entirely.

Early victories. I was only five years old when I won this race in Japan. (SUPPLIED)

Once I'd graduated to pedals. (SUPPLIED)

Me and Kai, ready to race. We were so cool. (SUPPLIED)

Robert de Wilde, the original pro with the number seventy-seven, came to Japan in 2006. He was also known as Afro Bob. We thought he was super cool, and he became Kai's favourite racer. (SUPPLIED)

Me with Sarah Walker in 2011, one of my heroes. Thirteen years later, she was the one to hang the Olympic gold medal around my neck. (SUPPLIED)

Our first European podium finish together as elite racers. This was in Verona, Italy. (SUPPLIED)

Channel 7's hero shoot of me and Kai. This was such a surreal feeling. (SUPPLIED)

Of all the TV shows I've been on, this has got to be the most fun one. Japanese comedy shows are something else! (SUPPLIED)

Kai and me, coaching in small town Nhulunbuy, far north Northern Territory. We have always wanted to give back to the BMX community and help grow the sport. (SUPPLIED)

Signing autographs after our coaching clinic in Belgium. (SUPPLIED)

Our first meeting with our manager Ryan Chipperfield. The start of a crazy journey together! (SUPPLIED)

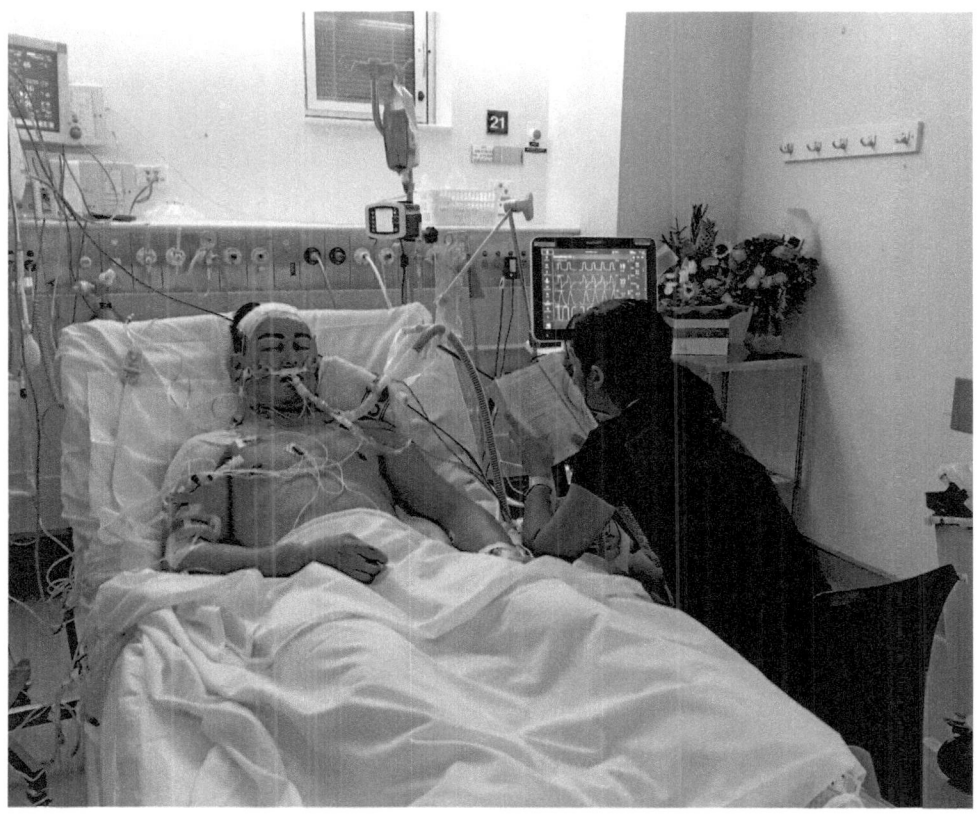

This photo carries a lot of weight. The support from the BMX community was incredible. (CREDIT: CRAIG DUTTON)

While Kai was in a coma, I read a chapter to him every day. (SUPPLIED)

Once Kai was well enough to visit home on the weekends, we had gyoza for dinner to celebrate. Every milestone was worth celebrating. *Left to right: Me, my dad Martin, my mum Yuki, Kai.* (SUPPLIED)

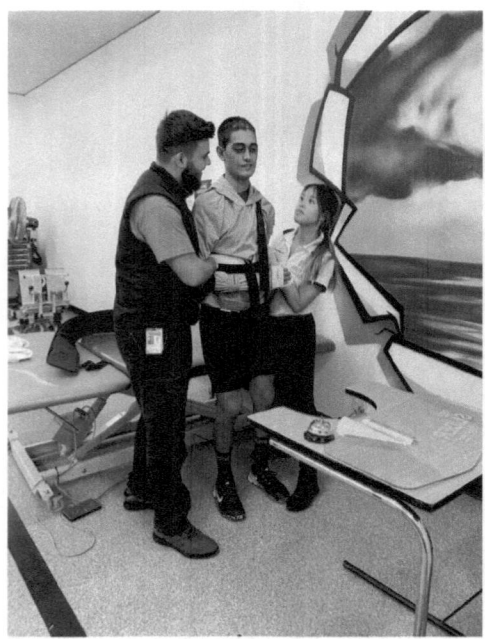

Everyone was ecstatic when Kai stood up for the first time after his brain injury. (SUPPLIED)

Kai timing my sprints for me. (SUPPLIED)

It felt like not that long after Kai's horrific crash that I had my own at the Tokyo Olympics. I had no idea then how badly this would affect me. (SUPPLIED)

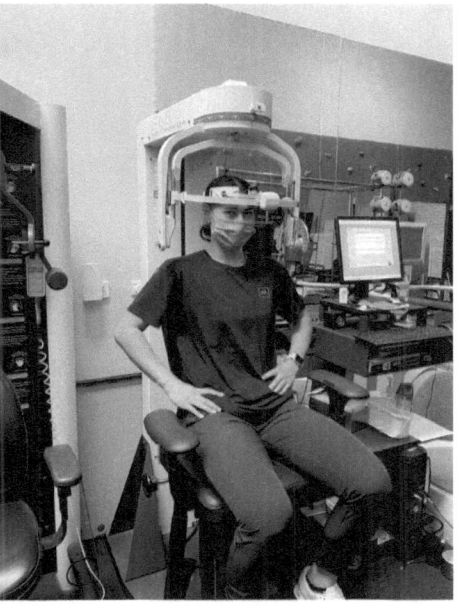

Strengthening my neck at the physio in Narrabeen. I hated doing these exercises, but I had real hope that this would fix my debilitating symptoms. (SUPPLIED)

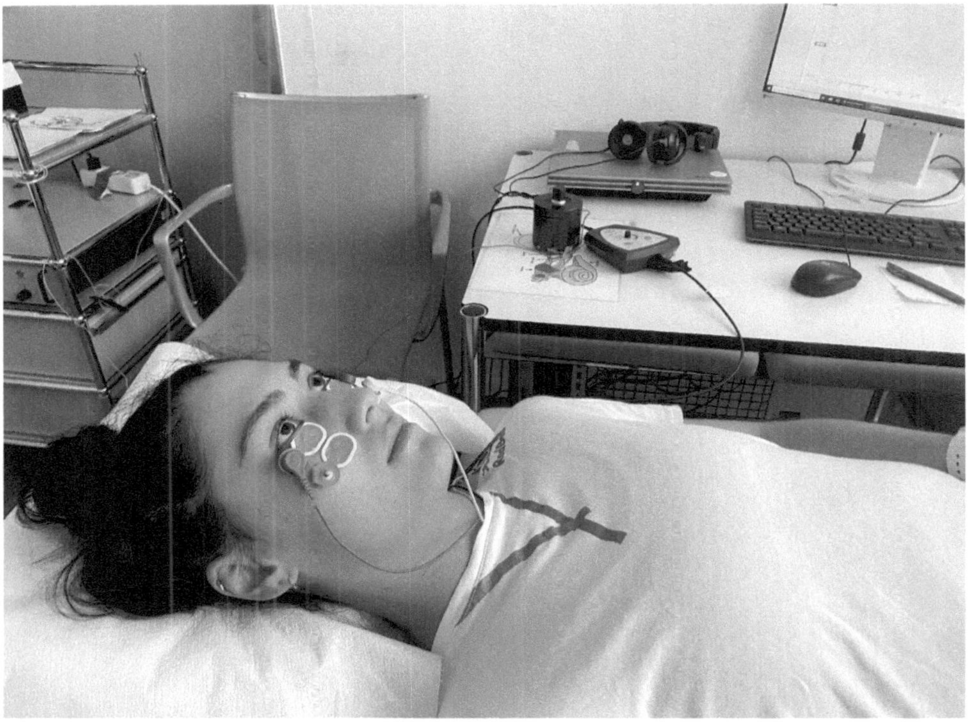

After all the medical advice I'd sought, it wasn't until I went to the Swiss Concussion Centre that my post-concussion syndrome was properly treated. The staff and facilities there were amazing. (SUPPLIED)

My brief foray into track cycling (left), then I began training like a track cycling athlete, under the guidance of my new strength coach, Toby Edwards (below). (SUPPLIED)

Once I'd recommitted to BMX, it was time for Project: Get Strong. I bought a new Speedco bike (pictured), rebuilt my team, and I worked on my mental fortitude – fighting the fear. (SUPPLIED)

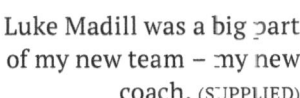

Luke Madill was a big part of my new team – my new coach. (SUPPLIED)

It can get pretty tight, racing down an eight-metre hill alongside seven other athletes.
(CREDIT: NAVADA PHOTOGRAPHY)

Weather has a huge impact on BMX races. Here I am, racing in the rain in Rotorua.
(CREDIT: NAVADA PHOTOGRAPHY)

The banked turns might look extreme, but they feel natural. This is Brisbane, and you can tell I'm the series leader by the red number plate.
(CREDIT: NAVADA PHOTOGRAPHY)

Winning the World Cup in Papendal in 2023 has to be one of the highlights of my career. Especially when Rom won as well! (SUPPLIED)

I was over the moon when I podiumed at Papendal in 2023, after crashing there one year before.
(CREDIT: NAVADA PHOTOGRAPHY)

Rom and I both came first at the Argentina World Cup in 2023. (SUPPLIED)

Left to right: Kai, me, Martin, Yuki. The whole family was there for the Brisbane 2024 World Cup. Whether from afar or in person, I always knew my family had my back. (SUPPLIED)

Left to right: Johanna Griggs, me, Kai, Martin, Yuki. This photo was taken in 2021, when *Better Homes and Gardens* came to film a backyard makeover at our family home. (SUPPLIED)

Rotorua, 2023. Rom and I know how to celebrate!
(CREDIT: NAVADA PHOTOGRAPHY)

From highs to lows. I had an incredible streak of wins and podium finishes leading up to the 2024 World Championships, only to come dead last. I still haven't recovered from the heartbreak. But it reminded me to stay sharp for the Paris Olympics.
(CREDIT: NAVADA PHOTOGRAPHY)

As I arrived in Paris, I realised I was now a two-time Olympian. But I wanted that gold medal. (SUPPLIED)

Of all the times to catch Covid, right before a chance at Olympic gold has got to be one of the worst. (SUPPLIED)

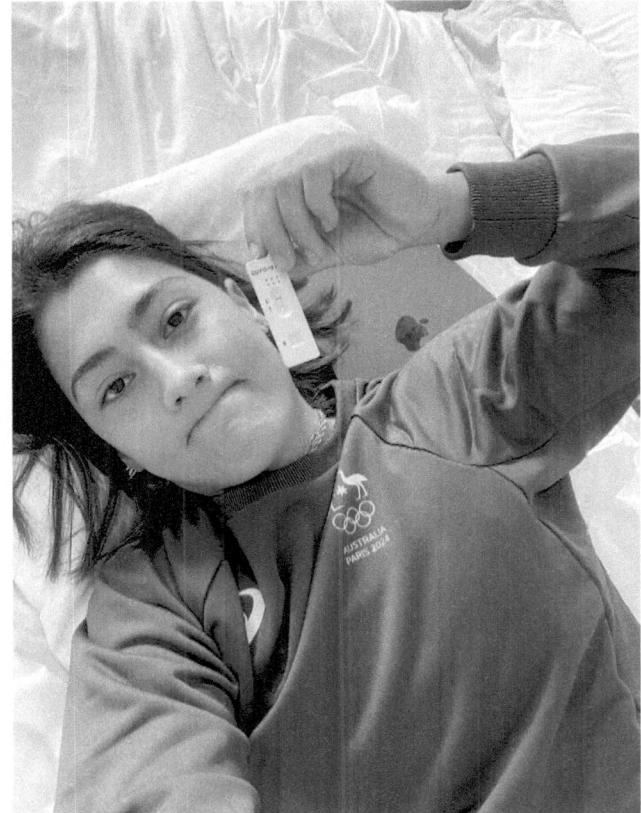

Me, racing at the Paris 2024 Olympic Games with the number seventy-seven on my number plate. (CREDIT: DAN HIMBRECHTS / AAP IMAGE)

I took this selfie in the car while being driven straight from the Olympic venue to the city to do media. It must've been close to midnight. The joy and pride I felt from this accomplishment, from earning this gold medal, is something I will never forget. (SUPPLIED)

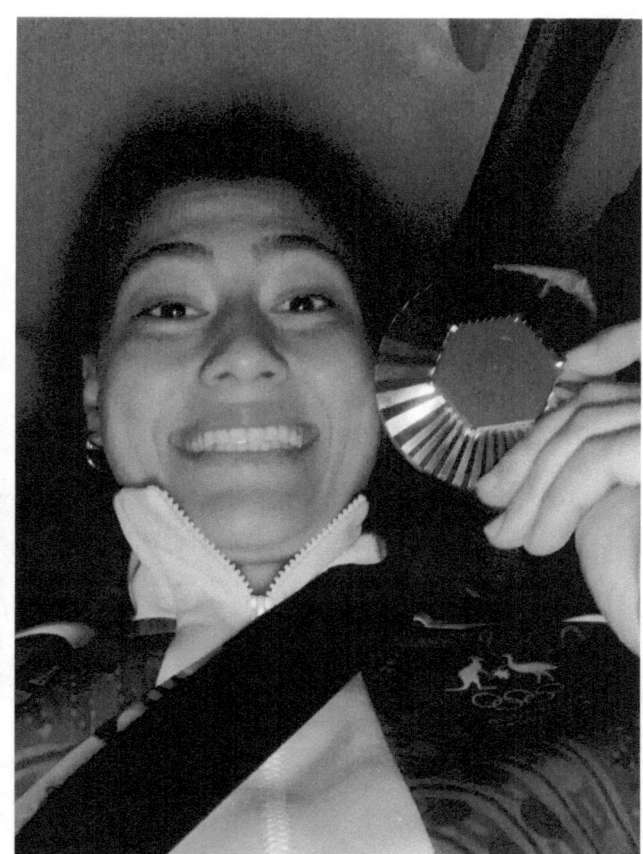

That's what happened with track.

This is a mistake, I'd think to myself. *What am I doing? Who am I to think I can make the Olympic Team in under two years' time?*

I spoke to my psychologist about it.

'Why do I think I could be better than all of these people who've been here for the long haul, people who haven't just waltzed in thinking they could have a go and smash it?'

Once again, I was leaping straight to the outcome and laser-focusing my definition of success on winning. I wasn't thinking about the process. I didn't seem to be too concerned with what I'd get out of the journey along the way. I needed to be there straight away. I think I thought that way since I'd never experienced a sport for any other reason. I believed that the only way to be happy with my performance was to win, to be the best in the world.

My psychologist told me that my goal should be to compete as a whole person, as a happy person who has her priorities clear in her head. That person shouldn't need a certain outcome. I shouldn't need to be the absolute best, to win the first time and then continue winning every single time, to be successful and to be happy.

I thought about what would make me a whole person. What was it, if not winning, that made me happy?

I loved Rom, and our life together. I thought about all the beautiful, fun moments we had together in-between all the chaos that was this year.

I loved that we had the same schedule, and trained together every single day. We understood each other because we were in it together. There was hardly any conflict, just mutual respect for one another.

I'm not sure I truly knew what happiness meant. But when I thought back to those small moments with Rom – when I most felt calm, content and at peace – it felt like that was the closest I had ever come to understanding it.

As I thought about the move to track cycling, I thought about what I was really giving up. *I am giving up on this amazing lifestyle. And how will our relationship change if I change sports?*

As these thoughts battled inside my head, I walked past the cabinet that housed the Sakakibara trophies from over the years. The shelves were overflowing, trophies for me and trophies for Kai stacked on top of each other with barely room to fit. National Championships, World Championships. My trophy from when I won a World Cup in my first year in Elite in 2018. The memories flooded back. I felt guilty for throwing it all away. I felt sad for nineteen-year-old Saya who had just won that World Cup. I had to tell her that this was the end of our BMX career.

I stood and examined the memorabilia for a moment. The birds were chirping outside, singing away the afternoon. I was giving up everything I'd built in BMX: my sponsors, my team and my fan base who had followed my journey. What would I be saying to my supporters who take inspiration from the fact that I keep at it, that I don't give up?

I had overcome brutal, recurrent injuries, I was resilient, I had a taste of what I could physically achieve, and now I was letting fear stump my progress? This wasn't right.

I picked up my second-place trophy from the World Championships in Brazil in 2006. This thing was heavy. I remember hardly being able to pick this thing off the floor when I was seven years old. That girl had a dream.

Was I really willing to leave my BMX journey here? Had I really given it everything I've got? Did I really give it my absolute all?

I couldn't lie to myself.

No, I hadn't.

Ever since I was a young girl, my dad always told me that it doesn't matter what the outcome is, what matters is that I try my best.

It didn't matter what it was, whether it was BMX, schoolwork, or a local swimming carnival. Doesn't matter what result I get, just as long as I give it my best.

I think that's why Dad was hard on me when I was younger. It wasn't that he needed to see me win or get good grades. He saw that I wasn't an all-in kind of girl as a default. But he saw what I could achieve when I did try.

I've learnt that lesson over and over again. If I look back on the countless moments in my life where I only gave a half-hearted effort, or didn't even bother – whether from laziness or a lack of self-belief – Dad or Kai would give me a push and almost every time, I realised that I could do it, I just had to try.

Whether I realised it at the time or not, I now know my dad was right. Throughout my life, I've always been rewarded for effort. Kai was a living, breathing testament to what it means to give everything. He lays it all on the line – every ounce of himself – so he can walk away with no regrets. Whether in training, racing, school, now rehab – everything. It's just who he is. He simply can't rest until he knows, deep down, that he's given it his all. Kai's the kind of person who always pushes for that extra set at the gym, or squeezes in one more full lap at the track. It wasn't required, but he would go the extra mile if he believed he could.

Walking away from BMX, at this moment, now felt wrong. This was what I'd been doing my whole life. This was Kai's legacy. I was a walking product of what Kai and I had built together. *And now I'm giving it all up just because I had one bad year? I'm throwing away another chance to be an Olympian just because of those voices in my head?*

Madness.

'Think of the successful people you most admire,' my psychologist said to me when I mentioned this.

I started to picture them in my head. New Zealand BMX

champion Sarah Walker. My late and great mentor Alex 'Chumpy' Pullin, Australian snowboarding legend. Colombian BMX Olympic Champion Mariana Pajón. Just thinking about them now, and how remarkable they are, totally gets the blood pumping through my body. Absolute legends. Giants, even among athletes. Heroes.

'Yes, but what stands out to you the most about them? First thing that comes to your head.'

It hit me like an instantaneous bolt of lightning. Yes, they were hugely successful. For sure, they were winners. But what I thought of was that the most captivating element of those people, their success aside, was that they glowed with joy.

They were confident. They were totally comfortable in their own skin. They were at ease with their place in the world. They always had big smiles on their faces. That's what grabbed me. That's what shone through so brightly.

They weren't afraid to be themselves, whatever that looked like. They weren't scared to be different.

I knew Chumpy. We were both Red Bull athletes. When I got to spend a bit of time with him he instantly became one of my heroes, someone I really looked up to, and I had the opportunity to be mentored by him.

He was incredible. His journey to the top wasn't an easy one. He carved out his own path, putting in the work and proving that an Aussie kid could go head-to-head with the best in the world. He was a snowboard cross athlete, which is a sport that has a lot of similarities with BMX racing. The jumps, the turns and the head-to-head, adrenaline-filled, high-speed racing to the finish line. I thought that it was the BMX racing of Winter Olympics. Action-packed and just so damn cool.

Chumpy was a three-time Olympian and the first Australian to win a World Cup event in snowboard cross, and then he went on to win two World Championships.

He was a natural on the slopes. Fearless, fast and technically flawless. But what made him stand out to me wasn't just that enormous talent, but his work ethic. He trained harder than anyone, studied every detail, and pushed himself to the absolute limit.

'You have to be completely in it. All-in,' he used to say to me. I still think of those words when I need a bit of motivation.

Even the tiniest details. Even if they seem insignificant. Go all-in. Mind and body. Those are the words he lived by.

But he wasn't all about competition. Snowboarding was his passion, but it wasn't his whole life. He was one of those people who had an energy about him that was impossible to ignore. He was a musician, a surfer, a diver and a guy who loved being outdoors and chasing whatever adventure came his way. He had this laid-back, easygoing vibe that made you forget just how fiercely competitive he could be.

Chumpy was also someone who had this infectious love for life. He had a rare ability to lift up everyone around him, to make you feel like anything was possible, and to remind you not to take things too seriously, even when the stakes were sky-high.

Chumpy was all-in in life. As I thought about what I admired about him, I realised it was the fact that he was a whole person and more. Just radiating with love for everything around him.

He died in 2020, aged just thirty-two, during a dive. Losing him was something no one thought possible. He was larger than life, and when you met him, he made you feel like you could do or be anything. He was in his element in the water that day, doing something he loved, and that's the only small comfort in the heartbreak.

It doesn't make it easier, but it speaks to the way he lived. Always all-in, always chasing the next wave, always embracing the beauty of the world around him.

I wanted to be like that. I wanted to be like Chumpy, and Sarah, and Mariana. I wanted to be passionate, dedicated and happy. I wanted to lift other people up. I wanted to bring them along on a journey with me and inspire them. And I wanted to do that with BMX.

I wanted to respect myself. I wanted to value my whole self, not just the part that wins.

I wanted to control my own life.

> **30 OCTOBER 2022**
> Helensburgh, Australia
>
> I want to race again. Who cares if I'm not the best anymore? What if I can just enjoy the lifestyle, improving myself every day, then make it to Paris?
>
> Obviously there's the added risk of hitting my head again. But is this a risk I'm willing to take?
>
> What if my goal in BMX was just to have fun? Do my absolute best and not force anything?

I didn't want to give up. I didn't want to walk away from this aspiration, this dream, and essentially admit defeat.

I realised in this moment that moving to track cycling wasn't my way forward out of this chaos. I had unfinished business to attend to in BMX racing.

But what about my head? What about looking after my head?

The doubt about my long-term health sprang up immediately. But spending that time in Switzerland allowed my head to be back running efficiently. It made me realise that I had probably been racing this past season with the enduring effects of my concussion in Tokyo in 2021, and then again from my head knock in West Palm Beach in January 2022.

Maybe my brain hadn't been working the way it was supposed to.

NOT DONE YET

Maybe, just maybe, the injuries I had sustained from the concussion had played a role in triggering negative emotions, or exacerbating the fear I was feeling. Maybe the concussion was the reason why I was so hard on myself. Maybe all those self-deprecating conversations I had with myself – that I wasn't good enough, or I didn't deserve to win – weren't actually me.

Maybe it was the concussion talking.

With a concussion, you can never know for sure how it affects someone. I know many people who have experienced emotional effects, like depression and anxiety, after obtaining a concussion.

The inefficiencies in my brain function were identified, and now after treatment I was back to neutral. I could look at my shocking 2022 season in a new light, and I had new hope that 2023 would look different.

For so much of 2022, I resented BMX. I'd directed so much anger towards the sport because of the things that happened to me. What happened to Kai, the concussions I'd had, the fear I felt.

But BMX didn't do those things. It was unfair of me to look for a convenient thing to blame. Blaming something that was out of my control was easier than dealing with the turmoil raging inside me.

If I had any chance of turning this all around, of going back to BMX properly and making it work, then I had to shift my thinking about the sport itself. I had to stop blaming it for the hurt and the heartache.

For all the grief I felt, BMX had given me so much positivity and opportunity. It had given me joy, friendships, incredible life experiences, amazing fans, a sense of financial security, and a whole heap of life lessons. It was how I met my amazing boyfriend, Rom. It had opened up the world.

BMX had offered me so much. And sure, it had asked a lot in return. But isn't that what makes great things worthwhile? Anything truly worth doing takes hard work. Nothing truly great comes from being comfortable. It's supposed to be hard.

There is always a cost to anything in life. Giving up BMX would save me the relentless quest against my fear. But that fear might be traded for regret. Being uncomfortable, being scared, having to be brave – maybe this was a cost I was willing to endure for all the epic things that doing this crazy sport rewards me with.

And then, when it is all over for real, on my terms, it would have thrust me onto an exciting new path. I could do something great with whatever I'd built by that point.

I had to stop feeling sorry for myself. Wallowing in pain and misery, thinking of myself as a victim and quietly admitting defeat, believing that there was no hope of ever getting better – it was such a toxic mindset to have. I hadn't been challenging it. I had welcomed it in and told it to enjoy its stay.

No more. It was time to make big changes and take steps towards where I wanted and needed to go. No more being passive. No more sitting on my hands hoping that everything would magically change. I had to take ownership of my situation.

Who did I want to be? What kind of athlete did I strive to become? I started to take steps to figure out the answers to those kinds of questions. I started to build a clear image of the new Saya in my head. Then, I decided to go find her. I committed to doing things every day to mould myself into the kind of person I could be proud of, I could love, and who was healthy and happy.

15 NOVEMBER 2022
Helensburgh, Australia

I went to Bruno Mars' concert tonight. I wasn't a huge fan of his, but wow. I was so impressed. His performance absolutely blew me away. Even being so far from the stage, he was able to capture my attention, engage me and communicate his passion.

He was so in his element, just so in the moment. He made it look effortless. He has such a fantastic presence.

He's doing something I don't – singing, dancing, playing instruments – but something about him really spoke to me. He was expressing his art in the way he wanted to. You could feel it so intensely. Passion. Dedication. Making the most of this incredible opportunity to share his talent, ability and art with tens of thousands of strangers.

> It's like he knew it was a privilege and he didn't want to waste a single second of it.
>
> I took so much inspiration from that. Passionate people are 'somebody', people who have this rare ability to convey something really special with no reservations. Authentic energy. I want to do that. I want to harness that same energy and passion to tell the world who I am and what I'm about. To express my own kind of art.
>
> How can I be more in my element? How can I share myself with the world?

A few days passed, and the more I let the thought of continuing BMX marinate in my head, the more it felt right.

As much as the thought of racing again scared the living daylights out of me, the thought of giving it all up terrified me more.

After my experience at the Bruno Mars concert, I started taking notice of talented performers all around me. Not in sport, but in other disciplines, like ballerinas, artists and public speakers. What they all have in common is that like Kai, like Chumpy, they are all-in. You can see it in their body language and energy. They've spent countless hours, training, practising, perfecting their craft. And they perform with their heart, no reservation, no hesitation.

That was the opposite of what I was doing in 2022 – racing with fear, doubt and zero self-belief. I wanted to become an athlete who rides and races with conviction and certainty. I want spectators to see and feel it when they watch me ride. I want to shift my inner beliefs so much that it radiates outwards. I want people to feel my passion. Whether I'm winning or not.

I'm not done yet.

Those words kept echoing in my head. They became ingrained in who I was, a determination that raged within me like a fire.

Kai never gave up. Even if he didn't get the result he wanted, he pressed on. He never let go of his dream. It didn't feel right in my body – in my heart – to walk away. He never chose to walk away.

I owed it to him and myself to give it another shot in 2023, and to do it properly this time. I had nothing to lose. It was an opportunity to reinvent myself. This was my chance to figure out who I was as a person and to be an athlete on my own terms.

It was an opportunity to heal my relationship with BMX and rediscover the fun side of it, what got me sucked into it in the first place.

I had to do it for myself. For the first time in my life, and in my career, it had to be just about Saya. What Saya needs, what she wants, and what she deserves.

So I got back on my BMX.

JUST GO

> **I'M NOT DONE YET**

CHAPTER ELEVEN

PROJECT: GET STRONG

At the end of 2022, I made the decision to part ways with my long-time bike manufacturing sponsor. It wasn't easy, and definitely not something I took lightly.

In BMX, having a bike sponsor is pretty much the norm at the elite level. Almost every top racer has a contract, has bikes and equipment supplied, and wears the badge of sponsorship like a mark of legitimacy. If you're sponsored, it means you're good.

So yeah, I was hesitant. I worried about how it would look. Would people take me seriously without a bike sponsor? What would they say?

On top of that, it meant a massive cut in my yearly income – this sponsor had been one of my biggest. While being part of the Australian Cycling Team would cover most of my travel costs, I still needed to figure out how to fund everyday life.

But despite all that hesitancy, deep down I knew: the partnership had run its course. It wasn't just me – it felt mutual. The relationship was built during the time Kai and I were both racing. And without him in the sport, it just wasn't the same anymore. It was time to let go.

Was it risky? Absolutely. I didn't have a backup plan. I was jumping ship without knowing what I'd land on.

But then again – what did I really have to lose? Not long before, I was teetering on the edge of quitting BMX entirely.

PROJECT: GET STRONG

I was fading into irrelevance. People were going to talk no matter what. So why not do what felt right?

I ended up buying a bike from Speedco. I'd been eyeing their bikes for a while and was curious to see what they felt like. There were a few differences right away – mainly that it had a carbon frame instead of alloy, which in theory offers less flex when pedalling and reduces power loss. The geometry was also slightly different. But more than anything, I just wanted to try something new.

Derek, the Speedco brand manager at the time, kindly gave me a big discount on a frame and fork. I still had other sponsors providing parts like the handlebars, wheels and cranks. I was putting together a 'dream' bike.

The frame and fork arrived in a box about a metre wide. I knew exactly what it was when the postman knocked on the door with it under his arm. With urgency I threw open the box and I instantly knew it was the one. Matte black with a carbon finish and a subtle logo – it had the look I wanted. I chose black deliberately, so attention would shift away from the bike itself and more onto *me* as a racer.

Rom helped me build it and the moment I rode it, it just . . . clicked. It felt right. Natural. Like the bike had been made for me.

This is what I'd been looking for.

What makes this moment worth mentioning is not how great the bike was, but simply that it was the first real choice I made for myself in my BMX career. It was a catalyst – a small but powerful spark – that gave me the confidence to start taking more risks and making decisions that felt right for *me*.

So much of my career up to that point had been doing what I was told. And in many ways, that made total sense. You've got a coach to fine-tune your skills, a trainer to get your body into peak condition. You're expected to trust them, listen to them, follow their advice.

But there were other parts of the sport, decisions that could've been mine, that I'd never questioned. I simply handed over the reins.

For a long time, Kai and I were on this journey together. We had a shared dream, and he was the leader. He took on the responsibility of getting us in front of sponsors, making the moves, setting our direction. I trusted him completely because I knew he had our best interests at heart. I was happy to follow, to do what he said. The bike I rode was sorted for me, handed to me. I didn't choose it. I didn't *need* to.

Choosing to buy my own bike, on my own terms, was empowering. I put my own skin in the game. It was investing in myself. Betting on myself that this will be worthwhile. It marked a shift. This was no longer someone else's path I was walking on – I was now carving out my own. I didn't have all the answers, but I followed a feeling. I gave myself permission to explore, to do it

PROJECT: GET STRONG

> **THIS WAS NO LONGER SOMEONE ELSE'S PATH – I WAS NOW CARVING OUT MY OWN**

my way. I stopped caring what others were doing or how things were 'supposed' to be done. This was entirely about me.

This led me down a path to change my helmet brand sponsor, too. I chose 6D, who had done extensive research in developing a safe helmet. You never know exactly how much a helmet can prevent concussions or traumatic brain injuries, but I felt the passion from the owner and employees of this company, and I felt safe to put my trust in their products.

I've come to believe that confidence comes from trust, and trust comes from evidence. In my pursuit of a comeback, I started making a series of choices, some small, some big, to rebuild Saya the athlete. And each time I made a decision and followed it through, I collected some more proof that I could trust myself. This was how I was going to get confident.

Because when you make choices for yourself, you own the outcome. If it fails or succeeds, it's on you. And weirdly, that's freeing.

David Goggins talks about a 'cookie jar' analogy. It's this mental tool he uses to pull strength from his past wins. The cookies in his cookie jars are those past wins, all the times he pushed through pain, fear or doubt, and came out the other side. Every time he endures something hard, he gets to throw a cookie in the jar.

Anytime Goggins finds himself in a tough situation, like during an ultra-endurance race when his body's breaking down

PROJECT: GET STRONG

and his mind wants to quit, he reaches inside his cookie jar and pulls out a memory of when he last found himself in a similar situation.

And honestly, I loved that idea. I knew I wanted to give racing another shot again, but I had no idea how I was going to get there. Filling up my own cookie jar was a start. The cookies weren't going to appear by themselves – I had to earn them.

That started the idea of Project: Get Strong.

Project: Get Strong was something I came up with, with the help of Scott Gardner, head coach at AusCycling. He wasn't my personal coach, but he oversaw athletes across multiple disciplines, including track sprint. Scott was someone who backed me when I told him I wanted to move to track – he was the one who helped facilitate my track sessions with NSWIS. And he backed me when I decided to pursue BMX after all.

Project: Get Strong was what the name suggests: a mission to get strong. If I wanted a successful comeback to BMX, I needed to elevate my game. The past two years had beaten me down, so I needed to physically, mentally and technically get strong – become a brand-new athlete to take on the world. But more importantly, I wanted to get strong to feel good about me again.

Throwing myself in the deep end the year before didn't work, and it wasn't the answer now. I couldn't go from level zero to ten and hope that everything would work itself out.

I needed to come up with a step-by-step plan. One that had challenges with the right level of difficulty along the way.

On New Year's Eve 2022, I packed up my little Hyundai ix35, and together with Rom, we hit the road. We stopped in the small Victorian country town of Bendigo for the night, we watched the New Year's Eve fireworks, and the next day we continued the drive. I watched out the window as long stretches of beautiful Australian countryside flashed past me. Almost three years ago, I was staring out at the same kind of rural emptiness on the drive to Canberra Hospital – back then, it made me feel lost. But this time, the emptiness felt different. It felt like a road to new beginnings.

After fifteen hours of driving, we arrived in Adelaide where I spent the next three months immersed in a new city, a new routine, and a new approach to training.

One of the biggest shifts was changing coaches. Phase one of my project was about getting physically stronger. So, I started working with Toby Edwards, a strength and conditioning coach who had been looking after the Australian track sprint team for years – and let me tell you, those athletes are *built*. It was clear from the start: I was in good hands.

I was totally new to his way of training. I liked it. Toby was all about getting strong and increasing muscle mass in the legs in particular. The stronger the legs, the stronger I could pedal the bike. He focused on getting the main leg lifts, what he calls the 'meat and potatoes', done really well. And the rest, what he called the 'gravy', he wasn't too fussed about. He let me do what I wanted in terms of upper body and accessory exercises. I had been training for years with gym coach James Tennent, including working closely on my technique of squats and deadlifts. I had built a really good foundation with James, which then accelerated my strength acquisition when I began working with Toby.

Scott introduced track cycling as a new element in my training. Even though I wasn't going to compete in track cycling, we both agreed that it would have a positive effect on my training. Track cyclists pedal on gears that are *massively* larger than what I'm used to on a BMX. The gears can be three to four times bigger. So, you need an incredible amount of strength and power to get the bike rolling from a standstill. The thinking was simple: if I could get strong pedalling a track bike, hopping back onto the BMX would feel effortless in comparison.

For the first time in a long while, I felt in control. I was in a new city, doing something that excited me. I didn't know if it would work, but it felt right. This was a decision I made for me. I was surrounded by amazing coaches, I felt inspired, and most importantly, I was seeing progress.

By the end of those three months in Adelaide, I had never felt stronger in my life. I was hitting personal bests in both squat and deadlift, and the physical changes were undeniable – more muscle, more power, more confidence.

JUST GO

To build confidence in my riding, I made challenges for myself each time I went to the track. If it was a gate start session, where I work on my start technique and reaction time, I would look at the times to make sure I was getting faster. I would get someone to video every start I did, so that later I could analyse all my tiny movements and how they affected my time. I learnt about my smallest habits, and changed any that were detrimental.

If it was a skills session, where I would work on my jumping and manualling at different speeds and on different-sized jumps, I would challenge myself to attempt new jumps – just like Kai used to when I was a kid.

---

12 FEBRUARY 2023
Adelaide, Australia

I feel so much better about myself. I am constantly being reminded that my love for BMX never existed in any kind of comfort zone. It's actually when I push and challenge myself to try new things that scare me, and things I really don't want to do in the moment, that I feel the most fulfilled.

It's fun. When the challenge element is gone, that's when the fun starts to wind down.

So, that's the new standard. That I challenge myself, whether it's a challenge to try a jump, a new line, go faster, and so on. It's a necessary element to my daily training. To be uncomfortable. To make myself pause and spend time in the discomfort.

PROJECT: GET STRONG

> I guess time away was good for my soul. A bit of distance from BMX made me realise that I perhaps wasn't done with it. And this new mindset – to just try to have fun with it and remove all the pressure – put me in a good place to at least get back on my bike.
>
> So, I did. And I really enjoyed it.

Seeing progress in my training helped stack up evidence that I *can* do things that scare me. And it piled on a whole lot of trust in myself. I could see the cookie jar filling up with evidence.

At the end of March, we packed up our life in Adelaide and made our way to the Gold Coast. There in Brisbane, only an hour away from where we stayed, is an Olympic standard track located in the Sleeman Sports Complex, that, in my view, is the best in Australia.

The second phase of my Get Strong project was all about applying the strength I'd built in the gym to the BMX track. It's one thing to be able to lift heavy weights in the gym – it's another to make that power count where it really matters: out of the gate and down the start hill.

That was the focus. I wasn't just chasing bigger numbers in the weight room – I wanted to be faster off the start. More explosive. More efficient. And over time, I started noticing the difference.

It was after only a few weeks' training at Sleeman that I noticed my start technique began to change, subtly at first.

I wasn't just pushing harder – I was using my body more effectively. The movements felt more connected, more stable, as if everything from my shoulders down to my feet was firing in sync.

With Toby, we were focused on getting my whole body stronger, but the priority was my lower back, glutes and hamstrings. I was doing way more deadlifts and posterior chain exercises to accomplish that. I could tell that doing those translated pretty well on the bike, and I could feel that my body was more stable out of the gate – meaning I was more efficient.

I felt faster, and my recorded times down the hill were faster than they had been previously. The training clearly worked. Another cookie went into the cookie jar.

However, every time I thought about racing, I still felt that familiar tightening in my chest – a looming sense of dread. I was still scared.

This was the third phase of Project: Get Strong – get mentally strong. I didn't expect to suddenly be confident and feel no fear, but I needed to take steps to feel confident *enough*. Confident enough that I could put myself on the starting gate and give it my all come race day.

During this time, I was trying everything. I read the books. Listened to the podcasts. Followed guided mindfulness meditations, visualisations. I even made vision boards. You name it – I tried it. But no matter how much work I put in, I couldn't shake the feeling: I wasn't ready to race, and I had no idea how to fix it.

I planned my first race back to be at the Oceania Championships in Rotorua, New Zealand, April 2023. I'd never ridden that track before, but from what I'd seen online, it was technical, had big jumps and demanded full commitment. One month out, I realised I didn't have the confidence I would need by then.

Then I remembered something from back in 2020, during the height of Covid. I'd done a series of performance coaching sessions online with Chumpy's coach, Nam Baldwin. I'd learnt so much from him, and that had a major impact on my training and my ability to show up for myself.

At this point, I'd already worked with several psychologists. Sometimes more than one at a time. Each brought something different. They helped me dig deep, reflect, and search for answers within. And while all those practices were valuable – and I genuinely gained a lot from them – there comes a point when you realise: you can't think your way out of everything.

I needed answers. Real ones. Not just tools. Not just ideas.

I reached out to Nam and scheduled a time with him. I needed some kind of guidance on how to get over this fear. The racing was coming up soon and I needed help.

During the session, I was holding back tears. I was trying to articulate my thoughts well so he could understand, but talking about it made my emotions run wild. It was hard to talk about, and at the same time I felt shame for being in this position. I hated that I had to go through this. *Why am I so weak? Do my competitors feel like this?*

But at this point I was willing to try just about anything, even if I felt embarrassed.

'Saya, you're lacking your purpose. Your "why",' Nam said. We had been sitting in his office for the past thirty minutes in front of a big whiteboard on wheels, like the ones you see in primary schools. He had been scribbling words, filling up the white space as we spoke.

He wrote 'WHY' in big letters and circled it.

And he was right.

My *why*. I hadn't thought about it in a long time, but it hit me – your purpose isn't just a motivational quote or something nice to say in interviews. It's your anchor. Your compass. It's what helps you find direction when you feel lost, and what keeps you steady when everything around you is uncertain.

Your purpose lights the path towards your goals. It turns effort into intention. It gives you a reason to embrace the grind, to push through feeling afraid, and it gives you perspective when you've hit a setback. When you know your why, you can face the hardest challenges and keep going – because you're not just chasing results, you're living out something that matters to you.

Without purpose, you're just floating – moving, yes, but aimlessly. Taking action without direction. So, when things get hard and scary, it's easy to give up. And that's exactly how I'd been feeling. I was doing all the right things – training, facing my fears, reflecting – but deep down, I wasn't sure what I was doing it *for*.

Finding your why doesn't solve everything, but it gives you something solid to stand on. And when the fear creeps in or the doubt gets loud, it reminds you what you're really fighting for.

What is my purpose? I had drawn a blank.

'I think your purpose is to face your fears – and show others how they can too,' he said.

And just like that, something clicked.

That one sentence was a light bulb moment. It cut through all the noise, all the doubt, all the mental spirals I'd been stuck in. *That* was the answer I had been searching for. It wasn't about chasing a podium. It wasn't about trying to be the best, or proving I still belonged. My purpose wasn't external. It was deeply personal. I was meant to do this terrifying, uncomfortable thing so I could show others – my fans, young riders, anyone watching – that it's possible to move through fear and keep going.

If I could do it, then maybe they could too.

That realisation changed everything.

I didn't need to win. I didn't even need to enjoy it. At least for now. For so long, I'd convinced myself that the goal was to love every second, to be light and joyful on the track. And when

I hadn't felt that in its entirety for the past few months, I'd freak out – thinking something must be wrong with me, with my mindset, with my motivation. But this new perspective stripped that all away. *The point was to show up anyway.*

The purpose was to challenge myself. To stand in front of the thing that scared me most and step forward anyway. Whether I smiled through it or gritted my teeth didn't matter. The purpose wasn't comfort – it was courage.

With that shift, my entire approach to training changed.

Every session had a new layer of meaning. It wasn't just about reps or sprints or lap times – it was about showing up for something bigger than myself. When I'd arrive at the track and the wind was howling, the fear would creep in. My chest would tighten. My thoughts would race. I'd feel the urge to pull back, to play it safe, to tell myself *maybe today isn't the day.*

But then I'd pause. Breathe. And remind myself: this is exactly why I'm here.

To face the wind. To face the voice that says, *don't*. To face the fear of failure, of injury, of not being enough.

I'd talk to myself. I'd go over my cues. I'd remember the evidence I'd built – the strength, the power, the progress. I'd anchor myself in the fact that I wasn't just training for speed or to win.

I was training for resilience.

PROJECT: GET STRONG

Sometimes, I'd still hesitate. But I'd go. One pedal stroke at a time. One lap at a time. I'd get it done. And every time I did, I added another piece of proof that I could trust myself.

That became my version of winning.

When April 2023 rolled around, I found myself standing at the start hill of the Oceania Championships in Rotorua. This was the first of two events I'd set for myself prior to the World Cup season as part of my mission to 'Get Strong' with racing again, both physically and mentally.

Although there is no such thing as 'Levels' in BMX, in my mind and in my trajectory, I saw this race as Level 1. It wasn't a high-stakes event. The competition wasn't as intense as what I was used to, and in theory, there wasn't much on the line. But the track? That was another story. It was technical, unforgiving and demanding. It required full commitment. And I didn't feel ready.

Race day brought yet another challenge: wind. The one thing that always got under my skin. I could feel it swirling around me as I stood at the top of the hill, waiting to roll into the gate. My arms were trembling. My grip on the bars was tight. And as I took off and jumped the first straight, I could feel the wind physically push at my bike.

I wasn't having fun. I wasn't smiling. I remember thinking, *I don't want to be here. I'd rather be at home, can this be over already?* The fear was overwhelming. And in that discomfort, one question echoed loud in my mind: *Why am I doing this?*

And then I remembered.

This is my purpose. This discomfort, this fear, was exactly where I was supposed to be. I wasn't here to enjoy it. I wasn't here to win. I was here to feel this, and to move through it anyway. That was the whole point of Project: Get Strong.

So I stayed. I took the leap, even though everything inside me wanted to run. Because at that moment, I had a choice: give it a try or back out and stay exactly where I was – stuck. And staying stuck was *not* part of the plan.

So I raced. Lap after lap. I rode scared, but I rode. And by the end of the day, I crossed the finish line as Oceania Champion.

But that title? That win? It wasn't the thing that made me proud.

What made me proud was that I showed up. I got it done. Not because I wasn't afraid – but because I was. I faced it. And I proved to myself, in a very real way, that I could do hard things, even when everything inside me said I couldn't.

I threw another cookie in the cookie jar.

10 APRIL 2023
Gold Coast, Australia

I've had this huge realisation that no matter what I do, I'm never going to be completely one hundred per cent ready. For anything. No human being is capable of that.

PROJECT: GET STRONG

Everyone feels at least a little bit imperfect. Even the most confident, the most capable and the most successful athletes aren't completely prepared for the challenges they face. They know who they are and what they've got, and they embrace it. They do what they know. They back themselves.

I need to do that. I need to start thinking — and believing — that I am enough. I'm good enough. I've done the work, I've prepared myself physically and mentally, and me, in this moment right now, is enough. I can do this.

I'm going to win. And I deserve to.

Conquering Level 1 meant I was on track to Level 2 in my mental process. Level 2 was a USA BMX national series race in Tulsa, Oklahoma in May, held just over a month after Level 1. The Tulsa race was going to be tough competition, a big track but low importance in results. It was the perfect next stepping stone in exposing myself to racing.

I was scared. The track was daunting, and the fact that there were more competitors only added to the fear. In Rotorua, there were only five of us lined up on a gate that usually holds eight riders. This meant there was much more space between each rider down the hill. Therefore, there was much less risk of tangling with another rider and crashing, which was comforting.

Here in Tulsa, there were eight of us. A full gate. The least amount of room possible. The distance between the end of your handlebar and the handlebar of the rider next to you would be no more than five to ten centimetres. When the gate goes down, it's a race to the bottom of the hill going fifty-five kilometres per hour. There is no room for error.

Exposing myself to racing again was one thing. But racing next to people in tight spaces, riding the eight-metre hill, doing the big jumps without hesitation? That was a whole other challenge. But if I wanted to race at the international level again, I'd have to be okay with this discomfort. At the end of the day, this *was* BMX racing.

Not long after my session with Nam, he introduced me to a mindset coach named Stuart Walter. He was also a hypnotist – which, to be honest, I didn't really buy into at first. I mean, what's a hypnotist going to do for me? All I could picture were movie scenes with swinging clocks and people falling asleep under some spell. I couldn't see how that was going to help me with racing.

But at that point, I was willing to try anything.

I walked into my first session with the vague hope that I'd walk out healed. That somehow, the heavy grey cloud of worry would be swept away in one go. That I'd look at a BMX track and feel nothing but excitement. That I'd be itching to race Rotorua.

That didn't happen. But something else did.

Stuart changed me in a way no one else had. He didn't wave a magic wand, but he gave me something more powerful – hope, strategies and courage. He didn't tell me to dig deep to find the answers myself, he actually told me what to do.

One of the biggest mindset shifts I ever had was born from something Stuart said early on in our work together: 'Winning is safe.'

It hit me like a truth I already knew – but had never had the words for.

He asked me, 'Where's the safest place to be in a BMX race?'

It was such a simple question, but it cut straight through.

At the front – where you control the chaos. Or at the very back – where you're completely out of it.

I knew, deep down, I never wanted to be at the back. That left only one option.

It made sense to me. Sure, I wanted to win, but even more than that, I didn't want to crash. I wanted to feel safe.

Then Stuart asked, 'What percentage do you think you're racing at right now?'

I told him, 'Maybe seventy per cent. My fear is holding me back from riding. And I'm scared to race because I know I can only be confident I'll be safe *if* I'm at one hundred per cent.'

And he shot back, 'So why not race at one hundred per cent? If you can choose to race at seventy per cent, then you can choose to race at one hundred per cent.'

He let that hang for a minute. 'If you raced at one hundred per cent, do you think you'd be in front?'

'Yes,' I said, without hesitation.

It landed like a tonne of bricks.

He was right.

I'd been holding back, not because I wasn't capable, but because I was afraid. I'd convinced myself that fear was something external, something I had to wait out or work around. But in that moment, I realised fear is a choice. And so is commitment.

I had more control than I thought. I could *choose* how fast I reacted. I could *choose* how committed I was. I choose my emotions, behaviours and habits.

Stuart didn't just challenge me to be faster. He challenged me to stop playing defence. He reframed everything. If I raced at one hundred per cent, chances were, I'd be in front.

And if I was in front, I'd be safe.

Instead of obsessing over the fear – over all the things that could go wrong – I started to focus on being safe by committing fully.

That changed everything.

I realised I couldn't afford to tiptoe into races anymore. No matter how ready I felt – or how scared I was – the gate was going to drop. The race was going to start. And the truth was, I was already putting myself at risk just by lining up.

So I may as well commit – fully and completely. Because holding back wasn't protecting me. It was only increasing the chances I'd get hurt.

PROJECT: GET STRONG

> **AT SOME POINT, YOU HAVE TO BE BRAVE AND JUST GO WITH EVERYTHING YOU'VE GOT**

And racing at one hundred per cent – that was my safest option.

Tulsa was a turning point.

That weekend, I lined up on the gate for my first race with a full gate of riders and my arms were shaking. Every part of me was screaming, *Don't do it.* The fear was deafening. I didn't believe I could win. I wasn't even sure if I'd be in front. But I told myself, *If I give it everything, at least I'll be putting myself in the best possible position.* And if it all went wrong? At least I'd have no regrets.

So I gripped my bars, took a deep breath and thought, *Stuff it – let's see what happens.*

I won that day.

Then I came third the next day.

I couldn't believe it. I *was* good enough. I *was* fast. It hit me hard – it wasn't fear that was holding me back, it was me. I had been choosing to let fear control me. That weekend taught me something vital: at some point, you *have* to be brave and just *go* with everything you've got before you can see what you're actually capable of.

If I had kept racing at seventy per cent I probably wouldn't have won. Worse – I might have ended up on the ground because I wasn't committing fully. And that would've left me with a false idea of where I was really at.

I walked away from Tulsa completely exhausted – but with a new understanding.

PROJECT: GET STRONG

It still felt strange that I won. Like it hadn't quite sunk in.

But it showed me something undeniable: I could win.

I was capable.

And that ability was always in there – I just had to stop getting in my own way.

12
12
12

CHAPTER TWELVE

ME VERSUS ME

It was around this time that I started working with coach Luke Madill. He represented Australia in the 2008 Games, the year BMX became an Olympic sport. Luke was a world-class racer who had won multiple Australian championships and had made multiple World Championship finals. I remember watching him race as a young girl. Back then he was known as 'Dr Smooth' because of how smoothly and effortlessly he raced.

I had never directly worked with Luke before, but I'd had many touch points with him over the years. We interacted when he was the coach for the National Development Academy team I was in when I was a teenager, he had given me advice at certain races, plus he introduced me to Red Bull as a sponsor. I also used to train at the full-sized BMX track in his backyard. I know, that looks like a typo. Before the Beijing Games, there were no tracks with an eight-metre hill in Australia. So, with the help of Red Bull and his sponsors, they built a BMX track in his backyard so he could train. It made the news!

Anyway, Luke maintained that track, created a club, and ran practice sessions each week. He let up-and-coming riders like me and Kai train on it, from when I was as young as fourteen until the property was sold and the track closed down in 2019.

When Scott suggested working with Luke, I was excited. I thought that we would be a good fit. Since we already knew each other, I was positive that we would work well together in no time.

ME VERSUS ME

I was already in France, staying there to prepare for the World Cup season, and Luke was in Sydney. He wasn't able to travel to my races, so our catch-ups would be over FaceTime and WhatsApp messages.

Which I was used to doing with my past coaches.

It had been rare in my racing career to have a coach present at every gym and track session. For the majority of the time I would have a program sent to me, and I would follow it. I would send videos and updates to the coach and do everything online.

It didn't bother me at all that Luke was back in Oz.

Our coaching relationship began as we were leading into the Turkey World Cup in June 2023, my next race. In my mind, this was Level 3. Big track, tough competition, high importance. As my plane landed in Sakarya, I thought about the fact that it had been almost a year since I crashed in Papendal and had my concussion. A full year since I'd lined up against these talented riders. It was a test to see who had been working hard over the off season.

I had been training. I had won the Oceania Championships and the race in Tulsa, but I felt the World Cup was another step up. I didn't know if my progress was enough, or how I would match up against these women.

During the practice sessions before the race, I felt so out of my element. I could feel myself comparing and ranking myself below the competitors around me. *They look fast. I'm so scared. I wish I was like them.*

In terms of strength and skill at that point, I was right up there with them. I should've known that by then after the races in Rotorua and Tulsa, but alas, I was there focusing on everything else but myself.

Like I said before, my fear wasn't something I could just switch off. It was still there and to be honest, I felt like I wasn't 'ready' yet. I wasn't one hundred per cent confident.

At the World Cups, riders select their starting lanes based on seeding. In the first round, lane choice is determined by each rider's international ranking. After that, it's based on the lap times from the previous round. The fastest rider gets first pick, and so on down the line.

I remember strategically picking my lanes before every race, seeing who my competitors were, predicting where they might pick and choose my preferred lanes. I was hoping so much that they wouldn't cut me off or take me out.

The inevitable race day came around on Saturday, and I was riding fearfully. I didn't commit and I was focused on others. I found myself stuck in the middle of the pack in the semi-final. I didn't make it through to the final. My day was done.

I messaged Luke who was up late, watching the livestream back at home.

'The bad thing is that I'm quite happy and relieved not to be racing the final,' I admitted.

I walked away from that day feeling like being a semi-finalist was probably the best I could do. It was fine, I told myself. I used to be on the podium, but not anymore. This is probably where I'm at. I was quite satisfied that I survived a race day without ending up at the medical tent. And even better, my day finished early, meaning I didn't have to put myself in danger in the final.

But on day two, I woke up feeling a little more confident. I felt calmer.

As I progressed through the earlier rounds, I found I had won the semi-final and qualified for the final. I discovered I had the fastest lap out of anyone in the semi-final. *What? First qualifier in the final? Me, really? There must've been a mix-up. There must've been something that happened in the other semi-final that slowed their lap times down.*

Nope, everyone had fast times. I was just the fastest. I couldn't believe it.

I chose lane one – a standard choice when you have first pick. And the Tokyo Olympic champion, Bethany Shriever, picked lane two. All I could think about was if she was going to be faster and cut me off.

In the final, I messed up my start, got cut off, got stuck in the pack and finished fifth. I was bummed.

In hindsight, I had already lost the race before it had begun. The moment I started questioning whether I deserved to be in lane one, I was already on the back foot. I had convinced myself that I was going to get cut off at the start. With that mindset, there was no chance I was going to win.

It was incredibly frustrating. I knew what I was capable of. I had the opportunity to succeed – and I let it slip through my fingers because I let my negative thoughts win. I hated the feeling of knowing I could've won if I hadn't allowed myself to believe in the lies my negative self was saying.

I am sure you've experienced many moments when you've let yourself down – not because you weren't capable but because you got in your own way. Maybe it was during sport, a performance, an exam or a presentation. You knew what to do, but you held yourself back. And afterwards, the regret set in. The what-ifs start playing on a loop inside your mind.

What if I just didn't care what people thought?

What if I had just trusted myself?

I don't know about you, but personally, these moments are the most painful. Getting beaten by another competitor sucks. But what's far worse is getting beaten because I let my negative thoughts win. I knew what I was capable of but I gatekept my own success.

At the end of the day, your mind controls your body. It controls how fast you react, how hard you pedal and how high you jump. Every mistake you make is a choice. Whether it was conscious or not. It's actually all within your control.

ME VERSUS ME

I realised I control me. Therefore, I have the power to control how I perform. I control my behaviours. I control my emotions. I control whether I hesitate or commit. I'm in control of it all.

So it was me versus me.

Me versus my greatest competition: negative Saya, trying to bring me down.

I didn't care who beat me as long as it wasn't me. I didn't care about winning the race. I cared about winning against the me that tries to pull me back.

That day in Turkey, I made it my mission to never let it win again.

The second stop of the World Cup series was two weeks later, held in Papendal. There was no denying it: in the lead-up to the race week, I felt completely overwhelmed.

It wasn't just the pressure of a high-stakes race weekend. Despite all of it – after everything I'd done to rebuild my mindset, to grow my confidence – the place carried so much weight for me. It was *Papendal*. This was where it all went wrong. Where I crashed. Where everything spiralled. Simply being back in the same hotel, walking the same halls, eating in the same dining room – it pulled me straight back to the dark days after my crash a year before.

During the practice sessions before the race, I had to learn a new track, because there were some changes made since last year. I surprised myself because honestly, I felt stronger than I had the year before. But it didn't change the underlying truth – I knew it could all happen again. One wrong move, one wrong moment, and I could be back at square one.

The day before the race is always the official practice session – your last chance to iron out the track, fine-tune everything, and leave feeling ready. But something just felt off. I couldn't put my finger on it. I had a press conference that morning, and afterwards, as I walked towards the track, I felt it – a heavy, sinking feeling in my chest. A sense of dread.

I didn't want to be there. I was terrified.

When I saw Rom at the track, I was barely holding it together. He could see something was wrong. He sat with me, trying to understand, but I was spiralling. I was having an emotional breakdown and there was nothing he could say or do that could pull me out of it.

Somehow, I pulled myself together enough to practise. The session itself wasn't awful, but I couldn't see it that way. I was being hard on myself – brutal, even. I kept thinking: *If I'm not perfect, I'll fall behind. And if I fall behind, I'm in danger again. I can't go through that again.* I needed to be out in front – not for glory, but for safety. I didn't want to crash.

Back at the hotel, I broke down. I let myself cry – really cry – for the first time that day. I'd been holding everything in, pretending to be okay, trying to manage it all. But I couldn't anymore. The fear came pouring out. And with it, the shame.

Why am I like this?

Why can't I just be normal?

After I settled down and tried to cheer myself up with a few episodes of *Friends*, I got up to the desk and opened my journal. I often used my journal in moments like this, as a tool to process my heightened emotions.

> 23 JUNE 2023
> Papendal, Netherlands
>
> I was trying so hard not to cry. I wanted to go home. I was getting more upset by the fact that I was losing to myself. Every day is a freaking battle.
>
> The gap between me and standing on the top of the podium is the battle inside my head. Win that, then I'm winning.
>
> I'm struggling though. I'm writing this and the emotions are coming up again. I can't stop crying.
>
> I hate this. It's so exhausting. I hate being upset.
>
> But actually, watching videos from today, despite how I was feeling, my first straights were strong! And I feel like I was only committing seventy per cent. So I have so much more in me. I have more to give. I've got this. I can handle this. It's mine. The battle is me against me. I am willing to take me on. Whatever 'she' throws at me. I wanna win this battle.

I knew I needed a way to get out of my own head. So, I turned to writing. I started putting my thoughts on paper, letting everything spill out. It was my way to process everything – the fear, the worry, the doubt – so I could see it clearly and think rationally again. Every time I did it, I felt a little lighter. Each word helped clear the fog, and with that clarity came focus. I'd set clear goals for myself. It wasn't about fighting the emotions – it was about making space for what was true.

I believed, and still believe, that the answers to my problems were already inside of me. I knew what I had to do. I just had to clear away the emotional clutter that was clouding my mind.

And when the next day came, I was ready. No more overthinking. No more doubting. I was ready to go to war.

My race day plan was simple: complete the race laps to the best of my ability. And what was in my way were my own negative thoughts. My focus was entirely on what I needed to do, and not letting my negative thoughts win.

By this time, I'd begun using my helmet as a physical touchstone for a mental strategy. When I put that helmet on, I wasn't just protecting my head. I was donning a metaphorical shield, covering my brain and warding off any of those negative thoughts, all those unhelpful distractions. I was shielding myself from the external so I could let my internal power go at full steam.

ME VERSUS ME

> **NO MORE DOUBTING. I WAS READY TO GO TO WAR**

When racing started in Papendal, the familiar feelings resurfaced. *Will she beat me? Am I going to crash? I don't want to watch someone else win.* But I reminded myself of the real battle.

Me versus me.

It wasn't about winning the race, it was about winning against my own limiting beliefs. I did not want to lose that battle.

I kept thinking like this through all the rounds. I was doing well, winning races and I ended up second qualifier for the final. All the while I was focusing on my mantra: me versus me.

Waiting for the final, I had to use every bit of strength to fight against those negative, fearful thoughts.

Just pull the brakes. No.

It's safer at the back. No.

I reminded myself of the feeling of disappointment after that race in Turkey two weeks earlier and what it felt like not to back myself. I recalled my frustration over that wasted opportunity and told myself, *Not this time.*

I trust myself completely, I told myself over and over as I lined up on the gate.

Just go, Saya.

I nailed my start and I had my wheel out in front. I was committed, attacking and fighting for that front position into the first corner.

ME VERSUS ME

I was leading! I was racing away, trying to stay ahead of everyone. Panic crept in as I realised what I was about to do. It was going to happen.

I crossed the finish line in first, and the feeling of relief was incredible. Then the disbelief. I freaking won! I won the Papendal World Cup! Holy crap, was this real?

One year after that almost career-ending crash, on the same track, I came in and won. Despite the way I felt, despite not wanting to do it, I trusted myself and won the race.

But most importantly I won against myself.

Me: 1. Negative Me: 0.

24 JUNE 2023
Avignon, France

I can't believe that actually happened. A week has passed since the World Cup in Papendal and I'm still so happy. It feels like I'm floating. Like, I am totally over the moon. It's crazy because I visualised everything happening – I imagined myself winning Papendal at the start of this year. I saw it all in my mind. And I kept visualising it every week for the past few months. Then, it happened.

In the quarterfinals, I decided to just go for it. I knew my gate was really strong and that fuelled me. I made sure to just push through the first jump. I cased it, but I got on the cranks straight away and holeshotted into the corner.

JUST GO

It's me against me, I told myself. Me against any of those old thoughts in my head. Me against any temptation to hesitate or to back down.

And I did it. I landed, I got the momentum I wanted, and I won the semi-final.

At the final, as I was walking up the hill to the starting gate, I could feel the nerves and anxiety rumbling away in my core. It was a lot. I felt really uncomfortable and I didn't want to do it anymore. I didn't want to be there. Those feelings are so destabilising. They almost hurt physically. They make it seem impossible to not run away and hide.

I put my bike on the gate, closed my eyes for a second, and told myself silently, I trust myself completely. It's me against me.

I had a great start and my lap was flawless.

When I crossed the finish line, I slammed into a wall of emotion. I had done it. I had won. I could barely believe it. I thought I would never get here again and that the best was well behind me.

It was almost like experiencing the sensation of relief for the very first time in my life. Against fear and anxiety, I backed myself, I realised my purpose, and I pushed through. I did it. I won.

Then Rom won as well. It was so amazing! I couldn't believe we got to share in this together. The stars had aligned.

It didn't feel real then and it still doesn't now, a week on. My Instagram DMs have been full of the most amazing, kind messages.

ME VERSUS ME

I'm so happy with myself that I managed to overcome the demons that have plagued me for two years now. I keep watching the video back of the finals. I've probably seen it hundreds of times.

It is real. It happened. I did it.

13
13
13

CHAPTER THIRTEEN

THE POWER OF LOVE

Rom is the best thing that has happened in my life so far. He changed my life without meaning to, and perhaps not in the way you might think. Or even the way that I thought he might.

How did we meet? Well, it's a story about a young man and his relentless quest to go after a girl he saw across the team pit area at a BMX race one day. It was back in 2017 at a World Championships in Rock Hill in the United States.

When saw me for the first time, he insists that he 'knew'. After that, he made a grand romantic gesture, straight out of a classic modern love story – he slid into my Instagram DMs.

I was eighteen and in another relationship at the time. I wasn't particularly interested in striking up a conversation. I didn't want the attention. But I was happy to shoot back a few polite messages here and there.

He persisted. Virtually, at least.

I was so confused by the fact that he would send me these friendly messages online but then totally avoid me at the BMX track. Not even a hello in real life! He told me later that he was painfully shy. I think in hindsight I was perhaps a little intimidating.

It was a year after he first saw me that we had our first real-life verbal exchange, at the opening rounds of the World Cup in France in 2018. I was on the podium, my very first World Cup as an elite racer. He was sitting nearby with two other men's winners, waiting for his turn to stand on the podium.

THE POWER OF LOVE

'Hey, congrats,' I said casually.

I had no feelings for him at this point. He was someone I had exchanged a couple of messages with, but who blanked me in real life. But I figured I should say something. Actual words. What a thought.

He looked up at me with this look of surprise on his face, and said, 'You too.'

It wasn't until 2019, after I had become single again, that we started to talk to each other at races. Then we'd go for a coffee on our days off, before a weekend of racing started. I was pretty hesitant about anything romantic developing, though. The thought of dating someone within BMX was one thing – what if we had a messy breakup, and still raced in the same circles? But on top of that, we'd be in a long-distance relationship too.

But no matter how blunt I was in my DMs back to him, or how long I left him on read, he was full steam ahead. By the end of that year, I couldn't deny my feelings for him anymore. I caved.

We had only been dating for five weeks when Kai had his accident. As I raced to Canberra to be by his side, Rom was preparing to fly out of the country. I wanted so badly for him to stay and to help me through such a scary time. But we'd been together for such a short time, so it would've been crazy to ask him to.

JUST GO

A month later, we saw each other again at a race in the US. Little did we know it would be the last time we'd be together for a very long time. Because soon after that, the entire world shut down when the pandemic kicked off.

We survived 362 days of FaceTime calls and constant messages. Through it all, we gave each other hope by saying: 'One day closer.' It became our mantra.

In March 2021, I flew to France to see him at last.

---

6 MARCH 2021
Paris, France

I made it! I freaking made it! I couldn't completely celebrate until I cleared customs because I was terrified there'd be some sort of Covid-related mishap. I almost wasn't allowed on the plane in Australia. It was such a mess of a process. But I'm here. I'm so happy.

Wow, seeing Rom again in person. For real. I couldn't believe it. It felt like a dream. I felt so many emotions and I couldn't get the words out. I just hugged him tight, not at all wanting to let him go.

He looked so handsome. So much more handsome than on FaceTime this past year we've spent apart. A small screen doesn't do him justice. Crap, what a huge chunk of time that was. But now we are together and it just feels perfect.

There was zero awkwardness, which would've probably been understandable, but it was like we picked up right where we left off. It felt like I was home. He feels like home. I don't want to let him go!

THE POWER OF LOVE

Rom is a pretty quiet and reserved guy, but he's also very sure of himself. He chooses to live in the present and there's hardly anything that can bother him.

'What's the point of stressing over something you can't control?' he often says.

As you can imagine, Rom's relaxed, unbothered nature has been so good for me. By now, you've probably gathered – after reading multiple chapters of my inner monologue – I'm a deep thinker. An overthinker, really. I spend most of my time living in the future. I get worried about what might happen. Playing out scenarios before they even exist. This was absolutely the case during those difficult few years while Kai was in hospital and I was racing with fear. Spiralling, overthinking, imagining the worst-case scenario – those were my norm. So having someone like Rom around, who operates with calm presence and zero drama, has been a much-needed counterbalance.

I'm sure Rom found this difficult to understand. He knew that I was an excellent rider, so watching me stress out about racing so much was confusing for him. He knew how hard I was training, since we trained together a lot in 2022. The thought of being overwhelmed by doing the thing we love, the thing that we feel like we were born to do, never entered his mind.

After Papendal 2023, Rom and I stayed in France together in preparation for the following round of the World Cup. It would

JUST GO

> IT FELT LIKE I WAS HOME. HE FEELS LIKE HOME

be held at Sarrians, in the South of France, a track I train on weekly – and knew I would perform really well at. But the night before, I found myself sitting at a hotel restaurant with Rom, desperately trying to hold back tears.

I was still scared of racing. Even though I had just won the Papendal World Cup, and had come second the next day, I still felt an intense sense of doom, like something bad was going to happen. I really did not want to race. Nothing could shift my belief in that moment that I wasn't up to it, even though all the evidence pointed to the contrary. I was freaking out.

I was hoping that Rom would give me a pep talk. I wished he would fix the problem for me, put both of his hands on my shoulders and tell me I had it in the bag. Talk it through with me, tell me I'm the best in the world, and that I had nothing to worry about.

He didn't do any of that. He never gave my freak-outs too much attention, which turned out to be a blessing. He didn't validate them, and therefore, he took away some of my fear's power. That was a much better approach.

'You know the track,' he told me. 'Go back to your room, write in your journal and focus on getting some sleep.'

Instead of talking about the feelings raging inside of me and creating an echo chamber between the two of us, and possibly exacerbating my fear, Rom brought me back to reality in a calming but firm way. He wasn't indulging my fear. He was subtly telling me that it was all a lie. There was no catastrophe. My fear was lying to me.

And most importantly, he believed in me. He'd seen the proof that I was good enough. I was great. I could do this. And he was right.

He gave me the courage to fix the problem myself. That contributed greatly to the process of regaining my confidence and my self-belief. That experience had a profound impact on my ability to bounce back in the moment.

I won the race the next day.

And I earned another cookie.

There was a part of me that felt bad unloading all of my crap onto him during race weeks. It was his race week too – not just mine. I was sure there were feelings he needed to get a handle on, and I wasn't giving him much space to share them. But he never dismissed me. He was always there to help.

I am so beyond thankful for that.

I have the utmost respect for Rom and so much gratitude for him. I'm so grateful that he chose me and continues to choose to be with me every day. But I'm also grateful because, without him, I don't think I would've had the courage to come back to BMX in 2023. I don't think I would've made it.

The power of Rom's love and trust was enormous. And partly thanks to him, I started to rediscover my love of BMX, and rediscover trust in myself too. Going through similar challenges and

THE POWER OF LOVE

being focused on a goal together helped me feel I'm not alone in this. No matter how hard it got, we were going through it together.

I've done a lot of reflection about the huge role Rom played in me getting through those difficult few years. The aftermath of Kai's accident. Tokyo. My lingering concussion symptoms. The total collapse of my confidence. The decision to quit BMX. The long road back.

Rom created a safe space in which I could navigate it all. His unwavering love, support and patience – so much patience – helped me to trust that no matter what happened in BMX, I had him. He wasn't going anywhere.

He gave me the space and encouragement to explore, and held out a safety net as I took my big leaps of faith. He believed in me when I didn't. He never told me how to manage my problems, what to do, what not to do. He just showed me that he was there for me, so I could be brave and figure it out myself.

No matter how many times I stumbled, no matter how hard I fell on my face, he would be there. Not a plane flight away, nor a drive, but right next to me.

That's what made all the difference.

CHAPTER FOURTEEN

SUPER-POWER UN-LOCKED

I had tasted success again at the Sarrians World Cup, but could I keep winning? Could I channel that success and become an Olympic gold medallist? That was thinking too far ahead.

If I wanted to succeed, I had to trust my bike, trust my training, trust those around me, and most importantly, trust myself. All those things were crucial.

I'd already worked hard to get where I was. There was no doubt that I was capable. I was physically in peak form, and I'd proved I could win again.

But there was a problem – a big problem. My mind still didn't believe I was good enough. I was still racing scared.

That became crystal clear towards the end of 2023.

After the triumph of Papendal and France, I came into two back-to-back weekends of competition as the series leader – four days of World Cup races held in Argentina. You'd have thought I'd be feeling good.

But still I remember practising on the days leading up to the race, watching the other riders and feeling the familiar thoughts unfurl.

Wow, they look so confident, I thought. *They look faster than me. Jeez, I'm nowhere near as good as them.*

Like attracts like. Whatever your mind thinks, it goes in search of things that are similar, or tries to find evidence to strengthen that idea. When those thoughts entered my head, if I didn't try to intercept it with a positive thought, it would go in search of other reasons I wasn't good enough or why the other riders were way better.

It was true. The more I thought about it, the more it seemed real. Those girls were way better. They were faster, they had more experience. In that moment I was swallowed by a spiral of self-defeating thoughts.

Accepting defeat at that moment, I slumped down on the seat of my bike, put my elbows on the handlebars and let my head fall, limp.

That's when I saw it. The red number plate.

At BMX racing events, all riders race with a plate that shows their own unique number, which attaches to the front of the handlebars. It's done so that commentators and announcers can identify who is racing as they are calling. Usually, the numbers are black digits on a white background, but what's cool about the World Cup series is that you get a red-coloured plate with white digits if you're the series leader. It signifies to fans who has the most points at that point in the season.

My red plate said seventy-seven – the number Kai used to race with before his accident.

In BMX, when you turn Elite and rank within the top forty, you get to choose a number that becomes yours – your identity on the track. When I first made it to Elite level, seventy-seven wasn't available. So I chose the closest thing I could: eighty-eight.

From then on, it was Kai and me – seventy-seven and eighty-eight. That's the number I raced with in Tokyo.

Then, in 2022, something changed. The number seventy-seven became available. I didn't hesitate. I applied for it without a second thought. At the time, I didn't realise how much it would come to mean to me. But as I started racing with it, something shifted.

'With seventy-seven on the plate . . . Saya Sakakibara.'

Hearing those words from the announcer made everything feel different.

Kai's career was cut short. And for a long time, there was a part of me that carried guilt – guilt for continuing on the dream we built together, without him by my side. It was just as much his dream as it was mine. If not more. He was the one leading. I was just tagging along.

But now, racing with seventy-seven felt like I was racing with him. That I was carrying him forward every time I rolled up to the gate.

Yes, it's a cool number. But more than that, it reminds me of why I'm here. It reminds me of him. Because without Kai, I wouldn't be the person I am today.

That day, as doubt swirled in my mind, I looked down at the red plate with the number seventy-seven on my handlebars and got a jolt. I was the series freaking leader. I earned this. I didn't only win multiple races to get this, I also overcame the very same thoughts, fear and lies that I was feeling in that very moment.

It reminded me that I had just won the Sarrians World Cup, racing against these same racers, only one month prior. My mind had decided to chuck that information in the bin. Forget how I won that race after having a complete breakdown the night before. Forget that I was consistently winning each lap without making any mistakes. Forget about all the cookies I had stacked up in the jar.

Even though I had stacks of evidence that I was good enough, my mind had a deep-rooted belief that racing equals crash and crash equals hit head.

My mindset coach Stuart had been telling me all year that racing equals fun and racing equals smiles. Racing equals smiles and smiles equals confidence. But I didn't believe a single word – even though I wanted to.

The thing about belief is that it takes time to develop and consolidate, and I had the Tokyo crash, the West Palm Beach crash and the Papendal crash firm in my memory.

So, inevitably, it was going to take time to change that belief to something else – let alone to the exact opposite. Just like your physical goals, changing your belief or way of thinking takes consistent effort and discipline. There isn't a particular way to achieve it, and just like your health, it's a constant thing that you always have to work on. Inevitability, you'll have a daily internal battle between who you are and the person you are trying to become. There was a war going on inside my mind.

When you get taken out in a collision with another rider, that sudden loss of control, and the split-second helplessness before you hit the ground, sticks with you.

It's not just about the pain of the crash itself, although that alone is enough to mess with your head. It's more that I had no influence over the outcome. Another rider clipped me, an event completely beyond my control, and everything abruptly shifted from picture perfect to complete disaster. I've had three crystal clear examples of this happening to me. And even with the many competitions I had raced crash-free in 2023, I was still fighting this belief.

For the 2022 and 2023 seasons, this fear of crashing remained my nemesis on the track. I couldn't get on the gate with another rider without feeling a sense of dread. In my head, it went like this: *I can't control what the other riders do. They could very easily cut me off and take me out midair if they wanted to.*

In my ironclad belief, as long as I wasn't clearly out in front, I was in the danger zone, completely petrified of the other women. In some circumstances, the fear was totally unforgiving.

My fear wasn't of heights or speed or something avoidable. I was afraid of racing. There are no lanes, there's eight athletes fighting hard for first place, and crashes are also an inevitable part of my sport. But once I had that first crash and first concussion, I couldn't forget it.

But when I interrupted these thoughts with a reminder of all the times I'd felt the same fear and powered through it, it shifted my whole perspective. I even reminded myself of the times I wasn't out in front but I was still okay.

It didn't mean I wasn't scared. My arms still shook on the gate. But I knew I could do it because I had done it before. All I had to do was trust my body. Trust that it knew what to do and commit like hell when the gate went down.

I knew that if I committed in that very first second, everything else would just flow. My body would go into autopilot and jet off. Being committed was my best chance of success. All I had to do was commit in that initial moment.

So, I put all my energy into that very moment.

I came second in that first day in Argentina, but I genuinely did my best. I committed, raced hard; the other athlete was just faster. I was happy.

The next day, I won. And a week later, still at the track in Argentina, I won both days. I became the 2023 World Cup overall champion, and I was the first Australian woman to do so.

I had won five out of nine finals in the 2023 World Cup season, and had come second in two of the others. I set the fastest lap of the weekend for the last three rounds. From the outside, it looked like dominance. But inside, I was racing with absolute terror.

Every time I lined up on that gate, I was still scared to crash. Still caught in that tug-of-war between who I was and who I was trying to become. The whole season felt like a constant push-pull – me, battling my own mind, trying to feel the slightest shift in how I saw racing, how I saw *myself*.

Even with five wins, that old belief that I wasn't good enough still lived somewhere deep beneath the surface. It didn't disappear with the acquisition of a trophy or a result sheet. Each time I crossed the line in first place, there was this strange mix of disbelief and pride. Like I still couldn't quite accept that I did that.

But by the end of those final two weekends in Argentina, something inside me did shift. I had just won the World Cup overall title. Not just one race, not just a lucky weekend – but the whole damn series. I was consistent. Reliable. Relentless. And that meant something. That wasn't by accident. That was earned.

And weirdly, when I looked back at the season, I found myself feeling grateful for the fear. The same fear that had paralysed me, made me question everything, made me want to run.

I felt grateful because the fear had also pushed me harder than anything else ever had. It stripped everything back and made me get serious. Focused. Ruthless in my approach. Fear made me pay attention to every tiny detail – because I knew if I didn't, I'd pay for it.

SUPERPOWER UNLOCKED

'AS LONG AS I HAD FEAR, I HAD FUEL'

That fear pushed me to refine every aspect of my riding. I broke down my gate starts and rebuilt them to be faster, sharper, more explosive. I focused on the first straight like my life depended on it – because in some ways, it felt like it did. If I could get to the front first, I could stay there. I could avoid the tangle, the chaos, the danger. I could protect myself by performing at my highest level.

Winning, for me, became a strategy for safety. The fear didn't go away – but I stopped letting it control me. Instead, I used it. I turned it into something that worked *for* me.

I had taken my greatest weakness and turned it into my greatest strength.

Fear used to paralyse me. I spent years trying to silence it, fight it, numb it. But it never left. No matter how much I trained, how many races I won, or how many deep breaths I took at the top of the start hill – it was always there, quietly waiting.

So instead of resisting it, I flipped it. I started to see fear for what it was: energy. And if I could learn to harness it, rather than fear it, then I had something powerful that no one else had.

As long as I had fear, I had fuel. It became my edge. My superpower. It sharpened me. Made me pay attention to every detail. It kept me humble and hungry. I wasn't trying to be fearless anymore – I was racing *with* the fear, using it to sharpen my instincts and push me beyond what I thought I was capable of.

And the truth was, I couldn't see the fear going away any time soon. Maybe it never would. But that was okay. Because I realised that no one else out there was carrying as much fear as I was and still turning up to race, like I did. Still pushing. Still winning.

That made me different. That made me dangerous. That made me unstoppable.

As I boarded the plane back to Australia, I thought about the next race, in 2024. And for the first time in a long time, I felt a flicker of something I hadn't felt in ages – *excitement*. It was small, almost too subtle to name, but it was there. A quiet spark. I still feared what was ahead. I knew the battles weren't over. But for once, I didn't feel the heavy dread that used to sit in my chest like a stone.

For the first time, I looked at racing and at BMX with softness. With light. I saw it as something that was good for me, not just something I had to survive. That tiny shift in perspective meant everything.

And as I sat there, watching the clouds roll past the aeroplane window, I thought to myself, *This is progress*.

20 OCTOBER 2023
Helensburgh, Australia

These past few nights, we've been watching old YouTube videos of BMX races – World Cups and World Championships from 2008 onwards. It's really inspired me.

JUST GO

There are riders who have been racing at the top for YEARS. A decade even. It's really amazing that they can be so good for so long. It fired me up to see how far I can go. And how long I can go on for. How long can I remain at the top for?

For the first time in a long time, I can see myself doing this until I'm old. It's a pretty nice feeling, given everything.

When I think about it, this lifestyle is freaking amazing. I love everything that BMX offers me and I'm so excited about all the doors this career can open for me.

I'm enjoying life. Really enjoying it. It could literally end any day and I need to remind myself of that, so I can ensure I'm soaking it up as much as possible. There are very few people that get to do this. I'm the healthiest, strongest, fastest and most successful I've ever been. I'm in the best form of my life.

But this won't last forever. So go soak it up, Saya! No more being scared. No more hesitating. No more standing back. This life is epic and it's yours. Don't forget that. You have almost everything you've ever wanted. Enjoy it.

Why not spend my time having fun and giving it my all? I can do that — I just need to think less.

There's no more room for overthinking. There's no time to worry and waste opportunities by getting in my own way. It's me versus me. The only person holding me back is me. I can succeed.

It's simple. Train hard. Work hard. Win. Because I deserve to win.

The thing I learnt about confidence is that it comes *after* doing the thing you're scared of, not the other way around. We often wait around for confidence to come before we take the first step. We have it all twisted.

Maybe reading another book will give me the confidence I need?

Maybe if I just talk to a few more people first?

Nonsense. These are all excuses we tell ourselves and all they do is stop us acting. We don't know we can do something until we do it.

Thinking back, I realised that during much of 2023, I didn't have the confidence to win, even though I ended up winning so many times.

I'd needed to race frightened. If I'd waited around just to feel a confidence that never would have come on its own, I would have been left paralysed – and none of those wins would be mine.

But I'd done it. I'd earned my newfound confidence, and now I could use it to propel myself towards the next challenge.

15
15
15

CHAPTER FIFTEEN

TOUGH LESSON LEARNT

When the 2024 season started in February, in Rotorua, the fear was still there – but this time, I welcomed it. Because I had a whole *library* of moments to look back on – evidence that I could do it. The past eight months had been the most consistent and most successful in my entire career. Since that race in Papendal, I had either won or placed second in *every single* World Cup final. I'd never experienced anything like it. To be honest, I was still trying to wrap my head around it. *This is me*, I'd think. *I'm the one who did this*. A multiple World Cup winner. Someone who had finished top two in the last ten World Cups. The cookie jar that was once empty was now overflowing. My fear wasn't holding me back anymore. It was pushing me forward.

Now, the challenge was no longer about reaching the top. It was about staying there. Holding my ground. Maintaining the pace for another six months until the Paris Games.

But strangely, I wasn't worried. I was nervous. I could feel it buzzing through every part of my body – just like last year. And I knew by now, that was a good sign. The nerves meant the fear was still alive in me. And fear was my superpower. It forced me to stay sharp, to push harder, to never settle.

But something was different. The fear had changed.

What used to be a fear of crashing had shifted into a fear of losing. Or more specifically, a fear of not committing, and then losing because of it. It was more mental than physical now – but it was still real.

I remember standing on the gate for the final in Rotorua, and the nerves hit hard. I hadn't nailed my semi-final, so I was fourth to pick my lane – stuck in the middle of the gate, surrounded on both sides. Not my favourite spot. No clean edge. No inside lane. I could feel the stress bubbling up from my stomach into my throat. I wanted to pull out. I was panicking, convincing myself I couldn't win from this lane.

And then I looked down the track, towards the finish line.

I pictured the moment the race would be over. What would it feel like if I'd let those thoughts get the better of me? If I gave up – not physically, but mentally – just because I was uncomfortable.

No way.

I remembered that sick, hollow feeling from the World Cup in Turkey last year when I didn't commit, when I let fear take the wheel. I would do anything to avoid feeling that again.

So I blocked it out. I focused. I committed.

I won.

That final, and the next day too. Picking up right where I left off.

It was the same success story for the following two rounds in Brisbane, two weeks later. The Brisbane race weekend brought an even bigger wave of stress, as I'd be racing in front of my home crowd – my family and friends had all travelled interstate just to watch me race. There was a Red Bull crew filming me for a documentary called *Saya Sakakibara: Ride to Redemption*. I also had another crew from *60 Minutes* capturing moments for their story that aired the following month.

I had so much media before the event asking me what my expectations were, and being told I was the crowd favourite. Don't get me wrong, I loved it. I loved the attention and how winning last year had captured the attention of the press. But subconsciously it was taking a toll.

I had the fear. Oh, how I felt it. I had such a fear of losing, but the fear of crashing came flooding back. I didn't want to crash in front of my friends and family. I didn't want to put them through the deeply buried emotions from the last time the World Cup came to Australia, now four years ago. I didn't want any of that.

I felt so much pressure that weekend, so much more than I ever felt before. This race meant so much, having the opportunity to win in front of a home crowd. I didn't want to waste this opportunity.

At the end of the weekend, my results were in: second place, both days. I was frustrated, but mostly I was just so relieved it was done, and that there were no crashes. I was safe.

A couple of months later, the last two rounds of the World Cup were held in Tulsa, in the United States. I was on a podium streak and on my way to winning another World Cup overall title. I desperately didn't want to lose.

I finished the weekend winning both days, and taking out the World Cup overall title for the second year in a row! I was so relieved more than anything. I hadn't wanted this opportunity to go to waste.

You might've noticed my language by now, when I talk about my motivation for pushing through and racing when I was afraid to – *I don't want to crash. I don't want to feel disappointed. I don't want. I don't want.*

All negative.

As much as Stuart, my mindset coach, would tell me I need to run towards something I want, I was still constantly running away from something I didn't want. In other words, instead of wanting to win, I didn't want to lose.

Even though they might achieve the same thing, they're quite different. Initially, I think running away from a negative can be a very powerful motivator. It can get you out of where you don't want to be, it's effective and reliable. But constantly running away from something is not sustainable and there comes a time in your journey when that needs to shift. According to Stuart, running towards something you do want has a greater pull than the push you get from running away from something you're avoiding.

See, the unconscious mind can't comprehend the word 'don't'.

Don't think about a blue car!

Saying anything you don't want just brings it to your attention, reminding yourself of something that isn't going to serve you.

So, changing my wording focused my attention on the result I was after. Think about the win, get out in front, trust the process.

For so long I was convinced that I was different. Because I had so much fear, I thought no other desire could ever be as strong as my desire not to lose or crash. I was counting on the fear to always be there to push me forward, so I didn't think about what I might want to chase.

Until the World Championships in May.

This year, they were held in Rock Hill, South Carolina, in the United States.

I knew I was the fastest one there. I wanted to win all three titles in 2024: the World Cup, the World Championships and the Olympics.

I'd approached the World Championships with my new positive mindset. I was feeling excited to race. There were no anxious feelings. I didn't feel stressed about it. I had this absolute conviction I was going to win. It was such a new and bizarre feeling.

And I was fast. I had the fastest laps out of everyone and I was riding well, until the semi-final. Looking back, I may have taken a little pressure off myself, since I let a rider from the US get in front of me on the first straight. I tried to catch up to pass her but I couldn't – I came second.

It knocked me mentally a little bit because that was not how this day was supposed to go. Was she faster than me? Was she going to be in front of me in the final too?

Crap, I thought. *I need a plan B to make sure I can pass her if I'm in this position again.*

I managed to wrestle with my mindset and by the time the final came around, I felt good. I didn't feel that intense feeling of fear or the dread of putting my bike on the gate that had plagued me for so long.

I really believed I was going to win, but in hindsight, I remember thinking that the win would just 'happen for me'. I thought I just had to trust. What I missed was actually doing the thing.

At the start of the final, I was late to react to the gate by a fraction of a second and that meant I was a little behind the other riders. I should've kept pedalling and raced at least to the bottom of the hill before assessing the situation. But no, I hesitated and found myself at the back of the pack, racing for sixth.

I panicked. I made multiple mistakes and I got spat out of the track in dead last.

Honestly, I was shocked. *I didn't win? I didn't even get a look-in. What happened? It's over? Shit.* Another disappointing

World Championships. How did I mess that one up? I blew it. There were no excuses.

I was devastated. It literally felt like the end of the world. I couldn't stop crying for hours.

The heartbreak of having an absolute conviction that I was going to come first, and then not even getting close, was awful. I felt extreme frustration and disappointment, knowing that there was no one to blame but me.

I didn't commit. Making a mistake sucked enough, but this was a whole other shade of terrible. Knowing everything was in my control and I let myself down was the most excruciating heartbreak I had ever felt. I'd really believed I was going to win.

My Worlds experience taught me an important lesson, but it came with some baggage. I knew I wanted to win the Olympics even more badly, and I still could, but my new strategy wasn't foolproof.

I thought my mental process was unshakeable. I thought it was my superpower. I had won nine out of twelve World Cups over the course of two seasons. I thought I had it all figured out. And now it seemed I was wrong.

After reflection, I learnt that I didn't feel that much fear. Almost none, compared to what I had felt in the past. In those final moments before the final, I wasn't scared of crashing, I wasn't scared of losing. And I didn't particularly have a burning desire to win either. It was this weird in-between with no push or pull. I had lost my superpower.

TOUGH LESSON LEARNT

It was like I was expecting to win automatically. I was expecting my brain to know what to do without me telling it. I thought, *I won every other final in recent memory, so why would this one be any different?*

In other words, I was letting it happen instead of making it happen.

'Me versus me' worked for me in the past but not anymore. Since I had less fear, I had to figure out a different approach. Fast.

The next race was the Olympics, in ten weeks' time. I had to fix my mental game. No more chances.

The clock was ticking.

Finally, after my heartbreak at the World Championships, I decided to change my motivation to running towards something I wanted, rather than avoiding a negative. Stuart had been telling me this for the past year but it was only truly sinking in now.

It was a quest in itself to work out what I wanted. Yes, I knew I wanted a gold medal. I wanted to win. Duh, that's easy. But that wasn't good enough. I needed to know *why* I wanted to win.

I'd spent a lot of time thinking about why I wanted to face my fears, but why I wanted to win was different.

It was something I'd never thought very deeply about before – even when I was faced with a similar dilemma before Tokyo, I didn't make it crystal clear.

JUST GO

"
I HAD TO FIGURE OUT A DIFFERENT APPROACH. FAST
"

TOUGH LESSON LEARNT

But now I knew for sure – I did need to know my why. And I needed it to be crystal clear. Because the next time I was going to be standing on top of the start hill for a final would be the Olympic final. I had to get this solid. No more cracks in my process.

Figuring out why I wanted to win a gold medal took me some time. I couldn't work it out. Was it for Kai? Was it to beat everyone? Was it for the fame? Was it for the money? None of these things really clicked. Eight weeks had passed, and yet I was still thinking.

I never thought about why I want to win. Is it because it feels good? Sure, it does, but does my whole journey to get here really boil down to just wanting to 'feel good'?

Since I was struggling to find an answer, I tried to think from a performance perspective. I said to myself, *Think about your final lap at the Olympics. What do I want that to look like?*

Fast, effortless, aggressive, flowy, fun.

If I was to be able to achieve that, what would I find, waiting at the finish line?

Pride.

That was it. I wanted to feel proud of myself. I wanted to walk away from my experience in Paris 2024 feeling proud of what I had done. I wanted to give it absolutely everything, leaving nothing out on the table. I wanted to feel proud of myself more than anything. This was my why.

JUST GO

In BMX, it's predictable and not predictable at the same time. Especially in an Olympic final, the favourites can choke and an underdog can pull off the performance of a lifetime. That's what I've seen in the past, at least. The pressure of the Olympic final can bring the best and worst out of racers. I was going to let it bring the best out of me.

> 20 JULY 2024
> Avignon, France
>
> I'm no longer running away from failure. I'm running towards victory. I'm running towards being the best. I'm running towards getting what I deserve.
>
> I know I'm going to stay focused. I know I'm going to go for it and I KNOW I'm going to be walking away from there having done absolutely everything. I know I'm walking away from the Olympics satisfied and I'm going to have a positive experience. I'm going to be proud of what I did. I'm going to be proud of how I handled everything. I'm going to be proud of how I stayed focused and GOT THE JOB DONE.
>
> Because I'm a legend.

At this point in my journey, my default emotion around racing wasn't excitement – it was nerves. Left unchecked, those nerves would take over and tamper with my whole experience. So I made it my mission to go out of my way to enjoy it.

That meant reminding myself, multiple times a day, to feel grateful for the opportunity. It meant smiling more than came naturally to me – so much that I went overboard. I smiled more than I ever have, because like Stuart said, race equals smiles, and smiles equals confidence.

When you smile, even if you're not genuinely 'happy', your brain starts searching for reasons to be happy. It shifts your mood, your energy, your whole state. And honestly? I was blown away by how well it worked.

I made it my mission to enjoy this Olympics. Since I was too stressed to enjoy Tokyo, I really wanted this time to be different. I was going to have fun.

Preparing for Paris was like nothing I had ever done before. I trusted my coaches Toby and Luke to give me the programs that I needed to be in peak physical form. I understood what they gave me and believed in it.

What was all on me was my mental preparation. Yes, I had Stuart, but he didn't give me day-to-day programs of what to do and how. He gave me ideas and I implemented them every day.

There are countless paths to winning a gold medal. There's no single 'right' way to mentally prepare or right way to feel in the lead-up. What worked for me may not work for others – and might not even work for me again. But at that time, it was the right approach.

JUST GO

I made a deliberate choice to believe, completely and unapologetically, that I was going to win. I went all-in. No doubts, no hedging – just a focused, almost delusional belief that I was coming home with gold.

It started with visualisation. I'd take about ten minutes to immerse myself in the moment I was chasing: the podium ceremony. Eyes closed, I'd mentally transport myself there. What was I seeing? Hearing? Feeling? I pictured the flags rising, the national anthem playing, and tears running down my face. I pictured everything in vivid detail.

At first, it felt awkward. The images were vague and the emotions felt forced. But with practice, the scenes became clearer, more textured. Eventually, it felt less like imagination – and more like memory. Like it had already happened.

Those visualisations rewired my brain to believe the gold medal was inevitable. And if I was standing on that top step, that meant I had already done everything necessary to get there: trained right, raced smart, trusted myself, stayed on my bike. I reverse-engineered the outcome in my mind until it felt real.

Visualisation wasn't just a tool to help me believe in winning – it was also how I worked through my hardest challenges. After the heartbreak of the World Championships, standing on the Olympic podium would mean I'd overcome that pain. I used it as fuel. That loss didn't break me; it lit the fire that helped me win Olympic gold.

TOUGH LESSON LEARNT

For the first time in Olympic BMX racing history, the Games track was open for training. Normally, athletes only get to ride it at the test event that could be held up to a year beforehand, and then during the Olympic week. But in Paris, the track was made available months in advance – any team could book time to learn the layout, drill their race lines, and get used to the environment. It was a huge advantage for those who could make the most of it.

So, two weeks after the World Championships, Rom and I packed up the car and drove six hours from the South of France to Paris. We committed to spending the entire month of June riding the track multiple times a week – learning it, piece by piece.

The track was big, fast and technical. When I first walked it, I was stunned by the size of the jumps – their length and height. This was the real deal. A true Olympic-level track. It demanded every part of what makes an elite BMX racer: explosive power, skill, split-second precision and next-level finesse. It rewarded riders who had both speed and confidence. If you could commit to the big jumps and execute them well, you'd carry more speed. There were safer options, but they were slow. The track was high risk, high reward.

This track scared me.

I'd ridden the track once before, back in April – and I'd crashed hard on the second straight, the most difficult section. That crash planted a seed of fear that stuck with me as I faced the track again in June.

The second straight demanded a precise nine-metre jump right after the first corner. It was all about timing. And every time I tried to hit it, I carried that fear with me.

During the month of June, I had worked through every other part of the track and was confident in most of it. Each week, I pushed a little harder, tested my limits, and made progress. But there was no way around the second straight. I had to face it. I had to master it.

This is where my visualisations became my lifeline. Because in those mental rehearsals, I had already seen myself on the podium. And if I was standing on that top step, it meant I had conquered every part of the race – including the second straight. That meant I had figured it out in training. That meant I would overcome the fear I was currently feeling.

It took four weeks. Four weeks of stress, fear, frustration, tears, self-doubt, and relentless effort. And finally, in that fourth week, I did it. I nailed the second straight – and I completed a full lap of the track.

Even with all the doubt I had about this second straight, I held onto one thing: the belief that it would work out in the end. It was part of the story I was writing. That belief kept me focused when I thought that trying was useless. Practising visualisation helped me remember that in every moment of uncertainty, the end was already written. As long as I kept persisting, I was going to be okay.

TOUGH LESSON LEARNT

Because that's what visualisation is. It's writing your own narrative before you go out and live it. It's truly a powerful tool.

Alongside the visualisations, at the start of the season Stuart asked me to start writing in my diary in a different way. I had been using my journal since 2019, recounting what happened in the day or using it to process heightened emotions. It had been something I relied on during the worst of times. But it was now time to level up.

He told me to write about my day tomorrow as if it had already happened. So, I had to write in the past tense.

> 9 APRIL 2024
> Avignon, France
>
> My new diary process doesn't involve recounting your thoughts or what happened in the day but just thinking about the next day and writing the diary for tomorrow as if it happened exactly as planned. It's been good. It makes you think optimistically, and it also helps you live the next day with more intention, knowing you've written about it.

I had been using this way of writing for the past seven months. It felt awkward at first, like anything, but over time, I started to get in the groove of it. I lived every day with intention, because I had already decided how it was going to go. I felt in charge of my destiny.

JUST GO

Diary entries on my training days leading up to the Games looked like this:

> **8 JULY 2024**
> Avignon, France
>
> I woke up with a smile and ready to take on the day. I didn't care about how I felt yesterday, I was just focused on today and getting the training done.
>
> I had a great session at the track. I warmed up well, and I did the second straight first go! I just trusted myself and went for it.
>
> I did some great gates. There was wind but I paid no attention to it. The focus and challenge was about getting closer to my best race pace. I put pressure on myself to get the job done. Regardless of how I felt.
>
> I was confident, I was attacking and it was such a good session.

By July 2024, I was ready. I felt confident about the track, I felt confident about how I was performing. I was nervous but ready.

I knew I was going to be an Olympic champion. I was unstoppable. I was going to blow everyone out of the water.

16
16
16

CHAPTER SIXTEEN

JUST GO

JUST GO

I'll never forget arriving in Paris for the Olympics. In all my years of travelling, it had never happened – until now. My luggage rolled out first on the carousel. First! It was such a tiny, silly thing, but I couldn't help grinning. I decided to take it as a sign. A very good sign. After picking up my athlete ID and some waiting around, eventually I was driven by a Paris 2024 volunteer to the Mercure Paris Velizy Hotel.

Because the competition venue was so far out of the city, the Australian Cycling Team didn't stay in the athletes' village. Instead, we stayed in a hotel that was closer to the track. I didn't mind at all. It made it feel like any other race – like a World Cup. Nothing out of the ordinary to implicate extra stress.

I sat in the front seat of the car and chatted to the driver. He was from Spain but spoke French, so I saw it as an opportunity to practise mine. We talked BMX, French life and my hopes for the Olympics.

'*Je vais gagner!*' I told him.

That means, 'I will win!'

The hotel itself was nothing flashy, but I had a king size bed, air conditioning and lots of room, so it felt like living in luxury compared to what I'd seen on social media about the athletes' village.

Sitting on the bed was a welcome letter from our Chef de Mission, Anna Meares, alongside a little Australian Olympic

Team boxing kangaroo plush toy. Across the other side of the room were two suitcases.

One was a huge canvas roller bag full of Olympic uniforms. Socks, t-shirts, dresses, raincoats, you name it. These were going to be my go-to clothes for the week.

I took some time to go through everything, making sure it all fit. That included the uniform athletes would wear on the podium when they won a medal.

Some athletes are superstitious. Some athletes don't wear it unless they've earned it. I'm not sure if I am, but after some consideration, I decided to take the jacket and pants out of the plastic and try them on. I stood in front of the mirror and took in the sight of myself in the green and gold from head to toe.

Closing my eyes, I felt the fabric on my skin and I played the Australian national anthem in my head. I could feel it as if it were really happening.

As I carefully took off the tags and placed the clothes on hangers and into the wardrobe, I whispered to them, 'Can't wait to wear you soon.'

The next day we had a day off, so the BMX race team went to visit the village to have a look around and have lunch at the dining hall.

The place was buzzing. Athletes and staff walking about and scooting around on city bikes. Naturally, you could easily spot anyone wearing the bright yellow Australian kit.

I was lucky enough to cross paths with some incredible Aussies. Meeting some of the swimmers was pretty special. They were so awe-inspiring to even see – tall, wide and proud. Wherever they went, they had so much presence.

It was a little daunting at times to meet these legends who I'd seen on television a million times before, who I'd cheered for. To see them in the flesh was special enough on its own, let alone having the privilege of being in Team Australia alongside them.

But I felt different being in the village compared with the last time in Tokyo. Yes, it was exciting, but I didn't have the desire to do the fun stuff like I had before.

There was a heap to do there, like going to Costa Coffee and getting a photo printed on a cappuccino, getting your nails done, or treating yourself to a baguette from the bakery.

I'd seen all the cool things on TikTok and Instagram, but I was there for just one thing: to win. Spending my energy exploring was not aligned with my goal. So I was so glad that I didn't need to be surrounded by the buzz, the constant noise, the sharing of spaces and all the distractions.

I was happy to head back to my hotel room, put my legs up and focus on recovering for a busy week ahead.

But amid the excitement, I faced a pretty dismaying setback.

On day three of being in Paris, I had the first of three practice sessions. I was confident I knew the track, so this practice session was about going through the motions.

JUST GO

It was all successful, all expected. I felt calm, confident and excited.

But that night, when I got back to the hotel, I started to feel a tickle in my throat. Maybe it was the dust from the track? Maybe there was some pollen in the air? I didn't think much of it. I remember chatting to Rom over FaceTime as I was getting ready for bed, since he was staying in a different location with the French Cycling Team. 'Oh, I think I'm getting sick,' I joked.

Except the next morning when I woke, it wasn't funny at all. I felt awful. Drowsy, dizzy and lethargic. My throat was sore.

Oh shit. I am sick. Wait, what does this mean? Do I tell someone?

I didn't want the team doctor to know in case he pulled me out of the competition, so I texted Luke and told him to meet me at breakfast.

'I think I'm sick,' I said.

'Oh really?' He sounded surprised and concerned.

'Yes.' I felt my eyes well up with tears. I tried to hold them back. I felt awful. My eyes were heavy and I just wanted to cry and sleep.

'Shit,' he said, under his breath.

A meeting with the team doctor Kevyn Hernandez was inevitable but, as much as I was dreading it, he didn't seem that worried. He handed me a Covid test and told me to do it asap.

The unopened RAT rested on the desk in my hotel room as I stared at it. I didn't want to take the test. *What if it's Covid? What if it's not?* I couldn't see either scenario being good.

I took a deep breath, opened the packet and stuck the swab in my nose.

Within seconds, both lines appeared on the test clear as day. I had Covid.

Kevyn was pragmatic. Surprisingly, he didn't seem too concerned. He simply gave me the medications I needed to quickly get back on my feet.

But I was panicking. This couldn't be happening. *Seriously? After all that, after everything I went through. This is how it ends?*

It was Tuesday and the race was on Friday night.

'Time is on your side,' Luke said. 'I suggest you skip the training tonight. Tomorrow, you have a full day to rest. On Thursday, the training is at night, so you have another whole day to rest before the last practice session. You know the track, it's fine to miss out on tonight's training.'

Outside, the Paris summer was starting to settle in, the heat rising slowly, while I sat alone in the artificial chill of my hotel room.

I was desperate for this not to be happening. I was so stressed, thinking about the worst-case scenario. *Maybe I won't race? Maybe I'll race feeling ill? What about my power? I won't be strong enough to get in front out of the gate!*

But I remembered how much I'd overcome in my BMX career. Enough to know that stressing about it wasn't the answer.

I needed to be the opposite of stressed. I had to be calm and trust myself.

This is going to be my gold medal story, I told myself. Even though every ounce of me wanted to freak out, I didn't.

Thinking I was going to win felt like I was going against the grain. But the alternative wasn't going to help me either.

'Useful delusion', I called it. *Stuff it. The worst has happened. Nothing I can do about it now.* I was just going to keep on with my visualisations and pretend that this was how it was supposed to go.

I did everything I could to recover speedily: I tuned out the world, lay on my bed, went outside and put my feet on the grass, took some vitamin D from the sun, drank my body weight in ginger shots, and otherwise followed the doctor's instructions.

I rested and watched a Japanese dating show to switch off my mind.

Two days later, the day of the last training session, another Covid test came back positive but I felt so much better. I felt fit enough to do the session, and thankfully it was allowed. I went out and did my best. I walked away from there feeling great. I was pretty much back to normal.

Close call.

Friday came around and it was the first day of the competition. I woke up feeling fine. *Thank goodness*. Today's Covid test came back negative and I was ready to go.

My phone vibrated. It was a message from Kai. He told me he was going to the track to watch me race. He told me he was so excited.

'Will you be happy for me when I win gold?' I asked him.

'You bet. But I'll be just as happy if something doesn't go your way because I'm really proud of you, Saya,' he wrote.

My brother. My biggest supporter. It meant a lot.

The format for these Games was pretty similar to Tokyo, except that instead of racing the same rivals each quarterfinal and semi-final, the heats were reseeded after each race according to the lap times. So, we would be racing against different competitors every time.

As I rocked up to the track for the quarterfinals, I caught myself thinking, *Wow, we are actually here. I am actually here. It's the freaking Olympics.*

It felt weirdly natural. Every time my mind drifted to overthinking or stressing out, I would remind myself that I'd done this so many times. It's literally the same task, against the same people.

It reminded me of something I once heard in the documentary *Victoria Pendleton: Cycling's Golden Girl*. Scott Gardner said of Victoria, when she was preparing for the 2012 London Games, 'She's not racing aliens.'

Nothing out of the ordinary. I knew what to do.

JUST GO

"**I'M REALLY PROUD OF YOU, SAYA**,"

The racing started at around eight o'clock in the evening. The sun was setting on what had been a hot Paris day, and a cool air began to surround the venue.

I walked up to the start hill and as I lined myself up behind lane one, I took a moment to look out.

The track was outdoors but it had a roof. The hanging lights shone bright on the perfectly groomed dirt track with vivid purple corners. I could see a number of broadcasting cameras situated around the track. There was even a Spidercam – those cameras that are suspended high above the track on four cables, like a spider in a web. I've seen them at football stadiums before, capturing the action, and I thought it was epic that there was one here to film the BMX racing.

The music was pumping as excited fans waved their country flags and bopped along to the beat. I could feel the mix of excitement and nervous energy under the roof. I scanned the crowd but quickly stopped because I didn't want to lock eyes with my family members, who were somewhere in the crowd. For some reason, I never liked seeing my family or people I care about in the crowd. Knowing they were there was enough.

I was ranked number one in the international ranking, so I was in the first heat and able to choose my starting lane first. I chose lane one. The crowd was getting restless; the race was about to start.

After the commentator announced the names of the riders, the music stopped and the venue went silent for the start of the race. I felt confident. The nerves were still there, but they weren't overwhelming like they had been in the past. They didn't weigh me down like sandbags. Instead, they felt more like small sparks of energy – a light, buzzing feeling that pushed me forward rather than held me back.

I want to feel proud, I reminded myself. *Let's just go!*

I nailed my first race. I blasted out of the gate and got myself in front. I could hear the roar of the crowd, the cheers echoing under the roof. I took the first corner and I jumped the second straight perfectly as if I had done it thousands of times. I was in the moment, everything flowed, I didn't need to think. I just let my body take over.

I had a clean lap with hardly any mistakes and finished the race first. It was the fastest lap out of everyone, and I smiled to myself. The first race is always nerve-racking so it was good to get it out of the way.

Next was the quarterfinal, which was seeded according to lap time. I was the fastest so I was in the first heat, with first lane choice. I kept it simple and chose lane one.

I won the next two quarterfinals in similar fashion.

Finishing that last race in first, and having nailed my runs, made it clear that I was the fastest one there. The only threat to me winning was me. And I knew that I wasn't going to get in my way. I'd done the mental work. There was no way I was going to blow it this time.

JUST GO

I knew tomorrow was going to be my day.

That night as I showered and wound down for bed, it was late. Almost midnight. I flopped on my bed, propped myself up with a pillow and leant back against the headboard. I reached for my journal.

I wrote:

> 2 AUGUST 2024
> Paris, France
>
> I freaking won!!! I am the Olympic gold medallist! I won it! I won the race. I did it. I did it.
>
> I woke up with a smile on my face because I knew today would be the day I won gold. I had a really good sleep and I was feeling refreshed.
>
> I stayed focused during racing. I kept my emotions away. I know how to deal with nerves. I focused on the task and not the result, which worked.
>
> I killed it in the semis, it didn't matter who was next to me, I put pressure on myself to get out and commit fully. I won every semi, no mistakes. Full commitment.
>
> In the final I lined up and I was focused. I was grateful for the chance to be here and for this opportunity. I told myself 100% commitment, trust, go.
>
> I nailed my start and I was fucking off. Running away. No one could catch me. I was gone. And I had such a good lap and I crossed the line first! And I won gold!

JUST GO

I smiled to myself as I put my journal down beside my bed. I could feel the thumping of my heart just imagining what tomorrow would hold.

I switched off the light.

The Olympic finals were held at night and around lunchtime, Kai texted me and told me he'd be watching from the grandstands along the last straight, near the finish line.

'You've got this,' he told me.

I rocked up to the track at six o'clock. I knew my final was at ten.

Four more hours, I told myself, smiling. *I've got this.*

As I went through the day, doing warm up and practice, I could feel my nerves ramping up a lot. I comforted myself with the thought that in four hours it would all be over. *No matter what, it's all going to end. No matter how I am feeling, it'll be done. So I may as well stay strong, resist the fear and make myself proud.*

My parents were in the grandstands, along with Kai.

Just like in recent competitions, the number I wore for the Games was seventy-seven. Kai's number.

With the number seventy-seven on my bike, I had won multiple World Cups. But I had always wanted to wear Kai's number and win something big. I had always wanted to dedicate a win to him. A World Championship or an Olympic gold medal.

Two more hours to go, I thought to myself as the nerves started to ramp up for the start of the semi-finals. I felt discomfort from the pressure and the unknown. I could feel it all around my body, pulsating through my veins, but I had to stay strong and stay focused.

As I lined up in lane one for my first race of the day, I felt comfortable. I felt like I had done this a million times. I could close my eyes and see how the race was going to play out. There was no reason why I wouldn't nail it.

Every time I had a negative thought creep up in my mind, I thought of my giant cookie jar overflowing with evidence to show that I was truly capable. I trusted myself completely.

Just go.

The gate slammed down for the first semi-final and I nailed my start. I raced down the hill and positioned myself out in front of the rest. Just like the quarterfinals, it felt fast, effortless, aggressive, flowy and fun. Exactly the way I had planned.

Soon, the semi-finals were run and done. I had won every lap, and I was the first qualifier into the final. At this point, I knew that no one could beat me. If anything, there could be a drag race on the first straight, but I had the advantage of having the most inside line.

In my mind, the race was mine. *I'm winning this thing.*

Thirty minutes to go.

The men's final happened first. And Rom was in it. The pits were mostly empty by this point due to everyone having left or having gone to watch the racing from the grandstands. The air was getting cool and the sky grew darker with the coming night, so I zipped up a jacket and stepped out of the tent to watch Rom on the big screen. He was in lane four. My heart thumped for him.

He's got this.

I saw on the TV that he nailed his gate. He had his wheel in front of everyone down the hill.

But he made a tiny mistake, almost invisible to the naked eye, when he came up a little too short on the first jump and washed off some speed. And that was enough for his teammate to cut under and make a pass into the first corner.

Rom was in third. I was cheering for him to pedal faster. I knew how much he wanted to win.

Suddenly, the race was done. Bronze medal. My first reaction was disappointment for him. It was all over.

But as I watched the aftermath, I realised the three French men had taken all three medals. Gold, silver and bronze. The teammates celebrated and the disappointment vanished. What an amazing achievement for Team France. And crap, Rom did so good too. Bronze freaking medal! That was awesome.

I was lost in watching the celebrations when I heard one of the Australian staff call out, 'Women final staging!'

Oh crap!

For a moment while watching Rom race, I completely forgot about my own race. I was late, trying hard not to panic. I fumbled to grab my helmet, goggles and gloves. I leaped onto my bike and made a beeline to the staging area.

As I was riding my bike to the bottom of the start hill for the women's final, I saw the other racers gathered there. I needed to pick my lane first, so they were all waiting for me.

I had this instant feeling of panic. My mind went blank.

Wait, what do I do again?

It was weird. I had never felt that way before. I think my brain had just realised the weight of this moment and stopped functioning normally.

My coach Luke was alongside me, walking quickly to keep up as I was riding.

'Luke, what do I do again?' I asked.

'Just fucking go,' he replied.

That was all I needed. I was back on.

The actual process of getting to the gate wasn't as quick as you'd think. There was a lot of waiting around. I had to wait to make the climb to the top of the eight-metre hill. I had to wait again about halfway up. Then I had to wait at the top for my name to be called before I could get into position. Plenty of time for nerves to go unchecked. But I stayed focused. *Just go.*

As I lined up behind lane one, I thought about the fact that I'd smashed it six times in two days in this exact spot. I was the *first qualifier* in the Olympic final. It was my race to win or lose. But this was exactly how I'd visualised it. The way the track looked, the way the grandstands looked – it was all familiar, like a comforting memory. It felt like I'd already lived this moment.

The only thing I had to do was allow my body to do what I've trained it to do, and just go.

I'm just gonna go, I told myself at the final. *I don't care if I crash. I'm just gonna go. Just fucking go!*

The camera panned to each of the eight riders as their names were announced starting from lane eight. The fans of each rider let out a cheer in support. There was a French racer that made the final, and by far, the cheers were the loudest for her. *Good for her,* I thought.

Each rider gave a wave and the camera moved on to the next. Lane one is always last. I gave my usual wave that I've done countless times. With my right hand I faced my palm to the camera and waved by quickly closing my fist and reopening it, like I was gripping then releasing an imaginary handlebar. I heard the cheers. All these people, here, about to witness a gold medal being won.

After the camera moved off to the side, the venue fell silent. The air damp with anticipation. The sun had completely set, and the dark blue sky surrounded the track. It looked like there were walls that enclosed the stadium. I took a deep breath and let it out like a sigh.

JUST GO

> # JUST FUCKING GO!

There was about a twenty second wait before the starter pressed the button to start the call, but that felt like an eternity. The pressure was on.

You could have a million thoughts in those twenty seconds. Good thoughts and bad. Helpful thoughts and destructive ones. I believe a race can be won or lost in that time, so I made sure I had the very best chance of being in the ultimate frame of mind.

Just fucking go, I told myself.

My mantra. It underpinned so much of what I'd learnt on my journey.

I had trained. I was in excellent shape. My form was unbeatable. I trusted myself, and my body, to do what it knew to do. All I had to do now was go, and race my heart out to the finish line, where the feeling of pride was waiting.

Just fucking go.

I felt no fear. Absolutely zero fear. Not even a flicker of doubt crept in. The dread of racing that used to twist my stomach, that used to steal the joy from racing, was gone.

This time I wasn't battling with myself inside my head. I wasn't hoping for it to be over. Instead, I felt something I hadn't felt in a long time: calm confidence. I was steady, present and completely focused.

And more than that, I was excited. Genuinely looking forward to racing this race.

I sat there with a quiet smile on my face under my helmet. I soaked it all in. The sounds. The track. The crowd. It didn't overwhelm me. It lit me up. Every part of me felt alive and I wasn't just ready, I *wanted* to race.

This is the Olympic final. Take it all in, Saya.

For the first time in what felt like forever, I didn't feel like an outsider in my own sport. I felt right at home. This was the feeling I had been chasing, not just performance but joy.

And in that moment as the starter yelled 'Set!', I knew I had found my way back to why I started this journey in the first place. BMX was fun again.

As I explained earlier, every BMX race begins with a random start. I knew that there would be anywhere between a half-second and a three second delay before the beeps, before the gate drops. I had to react perfectly.

I knew my race would be won or lost in that millisecond. Whether I commit, or whether I hesitate.

Beep, beep, beep, beeeeep!

I nailed my start. I was out. I pedalled as hard as I could, giving it everything.

The first jump was approaching, and I needed to nail it. The race was so tight, I couldn't waste even a millisecond.

I cleared the jump exactly how I wanted. I immediately got on the pedals again and fought for first place position by the first turn.

JUST GO

I held my position firm through the corner. At that point I was in front, and I controlled the race. That felt incredible. Everything flowed. I was pedalling hard, and I flew over the jumps on the second straight with ease. No landing a jump too short, no over jumping. Just perfect – like I'd done this a million times. It was easy, I felt free, I felt controlled, I felt in the moment and most of all, it was so fun.

By the second corner, I could tell there was quite a bit of a gap between me and the women behind. I let myself feel that, really absorb it for a second, and then it was back to focusing on trusting myself.

I trusted that I would commit, for every single second of this race.

It was coming into the last corner that I realised I was going to win gold.

As I soared across the line, I looked up and I saw Rom standing there cheering, fists in the air. How the hell did he get himself there?

Rom had just finished his race ten minutes prior, and was watching my race on the screen near the finish line, among the media in the mixed zone. Once he saw that I was going to win, he must've sneakily jumped the fence as I crossed the finish line. I am sure he was definitely not supposed to be there. But oh well, it made this moment one hundred times more special.

JUST GO

The look on his face made my heart leap into my throat. That's when I knew it had happened.

I did it.

I wanted to leap off my bike and fall into Rom's arms, but I was actually going too fast to stop. I slammed into cushioned mats and screamed, falling off my bike. I was on the ground and Rom's there, trying to get me on my feet. I finally got up and I was hyperventilating, in shock, excitement and just yelling all at once.

'You did it! You did it!' he yelled, as he put one hand on each side of my helmet.

I thought I might faint. I had put every bit of my energy into that final lap. Adding elation into the mix, I was suddenly super unsteady on my feet. I wanted to cry. It felt like a dream – the most beautiful dream I'd ever had. I backed myself, I trusted myself, and I went for it!

I spotted my coach Luke jump a fence and come running towards me, enveloping me in a huge embrace. I knew this meant so much to him too.

I jumped back on my bike, rolled onto the track and waved to the cheering crowd. I couldn't believe how happy I felt. I was absolutely on top of the world. To have had a massive goal like this, and to have worked tirelessly to accomplish it, to win, hit me like a tonne of bricks.

JUST GO

I wanted to win. I wanted to beat everyone and show that I was the best in the world. I wanted that moment, holding the Australian flag above my head and celebrating on the last straight. Photographers surrounding me to get the money shot. The clapping and cheers filled the venue and my ears. It was just as I had visualised.

I was taken off the track with an Australian flag draped over my shoulders. I slowly made my way through the mixed zone, talking to a whole bunch of different media, starting with Channel 9, the official broadcaster. I gave an interview thinking it wasn't live. No filters, just raw emotions. 'All I had to do was just fucking go, and I fucking went,' I said.

Then I got changed into my podium kit, the one I'd carefully hung in the wardrobe at the beginning of my stay in Paris, and then I had to wait to receive my medal.

That little stretch of time alone, for some quiet reflection, was when the gravity of the moment hit me.

'Holy crap,' I gasped under my breath. 'I'm here. I freaking won!'

I was reminded of the first time I visualised this moment back in 2023, with Stuart. As he talked me through the visualisation, I couldn't help but think about how far away it felt. Saya from 2023 didn't really believe she could do it. From a shell of myself, riddled with fear and self-doubt, to a proud Olympic champion, about to receive a gold medal.

It had felt so impossible. It seemed as though it would never become a reality. Not my reality, at least. But there I was, getting ready to climb to the tallest part of the podium.

It made me feel proud that I'd faced my fear. I had fought off every panic, every freak-out, every wave of fear. Not just on race days, but in the days leading up, too. I felt so proud that I was brave when I had wanted to back out. I felt proud that through everything, I didn't let go of this dream.

I closed my eyes and felt them well with tears. I didn't even try to hold them back. I let go.

I couldn't stop. Big, gulping sobs – some serious ugly crying. I didn't care. I just let it all out.

Sarah Walker, my idol, draped the medal around my neck. I've admired her for so long and looked up to her as a guiding light in the sport. She's such a fantastic rider but she's also a truly amazing person off the bike. It was so special that she was the one who put it on me. The tears wouldn't stop.

That day would've ended with waterworks either way. But there I was, sobbing for the right reasons, in the best of circumstances.

Mum, Dad and Kai came onto the track after I received my medal. We had a family huddle, arms draped around each other. It was so special that they could all be there and that we could experience this amazing accomplishment together. It had been a massive four years. For all of us, and in so many ways.

This wasn't just my win. It was our family's. And I absolutely believe that without Kai, there would be no gold medal at all.

If I didn't have Kai's guidance and encouragement, I never would've pushed myself to try new jumps and develop my skills as a kid. If I didn't have Kai, I never would've thought to get a coach and start training. If I didn't have Kai pushing me to do my best, I would've never had the high standards I have now.

Without Kai, I wouldn't be the athlete or person I am today.

This was our win. This was our medal. The dream had come true.

EPILOGUE

EPILOGUE

One morning in early 2025, I arrived at Sleeman Sports Complex in Brisbane for a training session. I was back into full training mode after months of media, speaking opportunities, school visits, photoshoots and awards nights. Despite all the media engagements I'd done over the years, this was a level I wasn't used to.

Alongside this busy schedule, I kept training, but at a slower pace. I was in the gym only a week after the Olympics, just to keep fit, and I rode local BMX tracks that didn't demand too much of me. There was no speeding down eight-metre start hills and no soaring over ten-metre jumps. I stayed within my comfort zone.

So, on this particular morning, it was time to get serious again. I was still a pro BMX athlete, and there would always be more races to compete in. My coach, Luke, wanted me to practise gate starts again – from the eight-metre hill. It had been eight months since the last time I had been on top of an eight-metre hill. Eight months since the Olympic final.

I stepped out of the car and gazed up at the hill. The Brisbane summer sun was beating down on me, and I used my hand to shade my eyes.

We meet again, I said to myself.

I started the session with a warm up. My usual routine was to spend about twenty to thirty minutes on the track, working on skills and cornering, before going up the hill.

As I started to ascend four flights of stairs to the top, my heart felt like it was going to jump out of my body. My chest tightened and my legs became heavy. My body was going into some fear response that I had never felt before.

What? What is this feeling? Is my body trying to tell me something?

Let's just squeeze the brakes and roll down, I thought. This is standard practice for when you've never jumped before. It helps you feel the steep decline and get a sense for how it would feel pedalling at full speed.

I rolled down. That wasn't so bad.

Yet I was still scared.

There was a breath of wind that blew on a diagonal from the back and to the right of me. The direction wasn't that dangerous, and the wind wouldn't be strong enough to push me off balance in the air.

But I didn't want to do it. I didn't *need* to do it. I could call it off and come back another day. When the conditions were perfect, and I wouldn't have to worry about the wind.

But Rom was here with me, and he was doing the eight-metre hill. Why was it so easy for him?

It's hard for me because I've been through a lot, I reminded myself. My multiple concussions, Kai's crash. I should just wait and do it next time.

But I didn't want to be the one not doing it. I didn't want to let myself down.

EPILOGUE

I went back and forth in my head like this. Trying my mental techniques to calm myself down, and to build up the courage to just go.

After thirty or so minutes – an eternity – of rolling down the hill, pulling the brakes and not jumping, I told Rom, 'Today isn't the day.' Tears were filling up in my eyes.

As I sat in defeat on a chair, I felt hopeless. I felt weak. I let the tears fall as I silently sobbed. I was beating myself up. *What am I freaking doing? Why am I so scared? Why can't I be normal? I am the Olympic champion, a gold medallist. I shouldn't feel like this. Champions aren't scared. Why am I crying? So pathetic.*

I could feel myself falling into the 'victim trap' again and I didn't like it.

Then something occurred to me, a sudden spark that burned those negative thoughts away.

I am not the Olympic champion because I don't feel fear. I am the Olympic champion because I fight through the fear. I'm frightened, but I just go anyway.

Yes. That's me. I may be fearful, I may be scared of my own damn sport, but I find a way and do it. I push through.

I'm brave. I'm strong. I'm determined. This was how I'd earned all those cookies in my jar. It's how I won this incredible medal. I'd embodied all these traits the last few years, and that wasn't going to change now.

So, you bet I picked myself up off that plastic chair, wiped my eyes, grabbed my helmet and started walking up that hill.

JUST GO

There's wind? *Just go.*

I am going to react as soon as I can.

I am going to pedal as hard as I can.

Be aggressive with my body positioning.

Push at the bottom of the hill.

Relax for the jump.

I broke the task into little sections and imagined myself doing them one by one.

I can do that.

I got myself on the gate with urgency. I had a wave of motivation, and I wanted to use it to my advantage. Do this jump before I changed my mind.

The gate went down and I pedalled hard. I jumped, landing safely on the other side.

The relief was incredible. I did it. And it wasn't as bad as I had imagined.

I was humbled by this experience. Truth be told, there's nothing fun about facing my fears. It's confronting. The satisfaction comes after doing it. And when I'm in the thick of fear, it's hard to remind myself of the rewarding feeling at the end.

By the end of the session, I had done a few gate starts, a few jumps. They were far from perfect. Ultimately, I barely worked on my gate technique, like Luke had planned for me. But I did the jump, and more importantly, I didn't let my fearful state of mind win. Just doing that jump one time was a way of showing

EPILOGUE

up for myself, trusting myself, and leaping ahead of who I was at the start of the session. I didn't quit and I gave it a crack. That was what mattered.

When I raced that Olympic final in Paris, and I felt zero fear, there was a big part of me that wanted to believe that that was the end of my struggles. I had conquered all. Surely, the demons were banished and would never return. I would love BMX for what it is, and my smile would never be wiped from my face.

That was far from reality.

The truth is, I don't think the fear will ever go away. Well, for me anyway.

But perhaps I've gone through enough to identify when it is worth pushing, and when it's worth coming back to try another day. Some days I am so focused and ready to tackle the challenge, and some days I just want to be anywhere but the track.

Most of the time, I just have to do it because I have no other choice. Not if I want to grow.

That's the nature of growth. Fear is an inevitable part of achieving greatness. My chase for success didn't end in Paris, nor did my doubts and fears. It is never-ending. As long as you are seeking something worthwhile, fear will be right there with you in the passenger seat. It's not your enemy. It's your copilot. As much as it can give you grief from time to time, fear is a valuable member on your road to success. It's a powerful motivator and it can be a superpower. We just need to find the courage to harness its power.

Winning that gold medal was everything I imagined. The elation, celebrations, attention and hype. The initial months after the Games were a mixture of relief, peace and disbelief. I couldn't believe it was all real. I still don't sometimes!

The gravity of this incredible accomplishment is only just starting to sink in as I write this now, almost a year after the fact. It took time for me to feel the full weight of my achievement and to believe it really happened. It wasn't a dream.

I've heard people describe winning as 'sweet'. For me, winning isn't something I feel on the tip of my tongue for a fleeting moment. It fills my entire body. I can feel it in my bones. It's a surge of energy that rises from my core. It's heavy, it's undeniably powerful. And it lingers, not like a taste, but like a presence.

It's deeply beautiful.

Once you've experienced winning, the discomfort and fear becomes a price you're willing to pay – because this feeling, this pure, fulfilling feeling, is addictive.

One day in December 2024, during a podcast interview, I was asked what I am most proud of.

What coincidence, I thought. *I was just reflecting about this.*

In 2022, I was someone who had very little belief in herself.

EPILOGUE

I thought I couldn't race a lap without crashing, or I thought that even if I had won a race, I hadn't deserved it. Even if my talent and abilities were there, I was beaten down by my own introspection.

Then two years later, I became someone who confidently thought she was going to win the freaking Olympics. Not just a fleeting thought, but an unshakeable belief.

What I am most proud of was my change in mindset. That shift in the way I viewed myself is by far the most fulfilling part of all of this. It's evident in the words I wrote in 2022 and the words I wrote in 2024, in the lead up to the Paris Games. The real fulfilment wasn't in achieving my goal – it was in becoming the kind of person who could.

I became someone who was resilient – not just through the obvious setbacks and losses, but during the quieter battles that others don't see: the daily doubts that crept in during training, the thoughts that whispered it would be easier to let up, to take the pressure off.

By deciding to not quit, I feel like I dodged a huge life mistake. And I am grateful for the journey that fear took me on.

When things get tough, it's not a sign to throw in the towel. You never know what's around the corner. You never know how close you are to something special.

Just imagine if I had given in to the fear. Imagine if I lowered my standards for myself. Imagine if I had walked away. None of this would have happened. BMX wouldn't have been front and centre of the news stories from the Paris Olympics. You certainly wouldn't be reading this book.

My journey is a testament to what's possible when you find a way to persevere through challenges and rough patches. It's about aiming for something you want, even if it feels unreachable at the time. And it's about understanding that the road to success is messy. Really messy. But it doesn't mean you're not on the right track.

My journey is proof that the toughest obstacle you'll ever have to overcome is not injuries or losses.

It's *you*.

The negative voice in my head told me so often that I was not good enough, strong enough, skilled enough or deserving enough. But it was wrong. And it's up to me to do something about it. To ignore that voice, to disagree with that voice. That's the biggest battle I'll ever face.

Once you overcome your biggest obstacle, the possibilities of what you can achieve are endless.

BMX racing is still a niche sport, but compared to when I was a kid, the sport has had incredible growth. When I was young, I didn't see BMX on TV, there were certainly no books about BMX racing athletes, and despite being in the Olympics since 2008, hardly anybody knew it was an Olympic sport. It was

EPILOGUE

"THAT'S THE BIGGEST BATTLE I'LL EVER FACE"

viewed as a bit of a casual, backyard sport that kids do on the weekend. Not many people knew about it, and if I told people I did BMX, I would get comments like, 'Oh cool, can you do a backflip?'

BMX racing had so much coverage at the Paris Games, which put the sport in front of a huge population who had never seen it before. It feels incredible to play a role in spreading awareness of this sport and contribute to its momentum.

Coming home with the gold medal really opened my eyes to just how much of an impact I can have with young people. I've met so many kids and have been totally blown away by their enthusiasm. And not just from those within the BMX community.

I've loved hearing from people about how my story has resonated with them in some way.

After having been on this journey and having won, not just gold but my mental battle too, now I want to contribute to the next generation of BMX racers and see them succeed. For the riders themselves and for the continued growth of the sport.

In late 2024, I met a family at the BMX National Championships in Perth. They were there to watch a young relative of theirs compete. I posed for a photo with them and signed an autograph before the dad dropped a massive bombshell that still gives me goosebumps whenever I think about it.

EPILOGUE

'You brought my daughter back to BMX,' he told me, beaming with pride. 'She had quit. Walked away. Watching you in Paris, it inspired her to get back on the bike and here she is now.'

That was such a special moment for me.

I love the idea of being an inspiration to someone. I like knowing that what I've faced, endured and overcome, and what I've been able to achieve as a result, is something people look up to.

But it's also surreal to think about. It's a little daunting too, if I'm honest. I can imagine myself, not too far down the track – but almost an eternity in the world of elite sports – lining up on the gate for a World Cup, World Championships or even an Olympic final, going up against someone who watched me win in Paris when she was a little girl.

She's going to challenge me in ways I didn't even know were possible. She's going to be right at my heels, trying to dominate, trying to prove herself, bringing her fire and grit, all in a bid to beat me.

She's going to be my absolute worst nightmare.

I can't wait.

ACKNOWL-
EDGEMENTS

ACKNOWLEDGEMENTS

When I was presented with an opportunity to write a book only a couple of months after I won gold in Paris, I was overjoyed by the idea. But then came the realisation that 'I', as in me, Saya, is going to write a book. I'm no author, and I couldn't imagine how I could even make a start.

Yet here we are. I wrote a book! But it would never have been possible without a team of incredible individuals who worked tirelessly to help bring my story out of my mind and into your hands.

Firstly, I'd like to acknowledge my manager, Ryan Chipperfield, for handling everything on the commercial side of being an elite athlete – and for making this book possible. I have truly valued having someone who knows me, my story, and my aspirations; someone I could trust, who was there at every step of the process. He is a wizard at what he does and I want to acknowledge everything he has done for Kai and me over the years.

There would be no book without the team at Simon & Schuster, the publishers of this book. They are an incredible bunch of enthusiastic individuals who just love telling stories. They made the overwhelming process of writing a book stress free and truly enjoyable. A special mention to Emma Nolan, Jade Gould and my editor Jarred Noulton.

To my aunty Catherine Ward, who I turned to throughout the book process for honest and thoughtful feedback. Having the perspective of someone who knows me, but isn't fully immersed in my world – and who happens to be a true bookworm – was invaluable. She offered insights I hadn't considered and helped to ensure I wrote about BMX in a way that anyone could understand.

A special thank you goes to Joh Griggs, who is a fabulous woman who kindly wrote the foreword for this book. It is an absolute pleasure to know Joh and she has been so supportive of Kai and me since we first met back in 2019.

I'd like to take this opportunity to mention some people who I believe were instrumental in reaching where I am now.

My coaches Luke Madill and Toby Edwards, for the time and effort they put in to get me in the best shape possible for racing. Their level of expertise is outstanding and they are just simply great people to work with.

To my mindset coach Stuart Walter. Our work together has been life-changing, I owe a lot of my growth to him.

To Rom. My saviour. I don't know what I would've done without him. Going through this journey together was massive in more ways than one. We understand each other, we go through the struggles together and celebrate together. I know I must've given him grief in many moments along the way, but I am so grateful.

My parents, Martin and Yuki. For their unconditional support. They were always there. My parents would stay up all hours of

ACKNOWLEDGEMENTS

the night to watch me race. From the day I started scooting away on my bike with no training wheels, they dared to allow Kai and me to dream big.

Last but not least, Kai. The beginning of all of this. The foundation of what I've been able to build and my biggest cheerleader as I chased our dream. I hope this book shows just how much he had a positive impact on me and I can't wait to support him with whatever he sets his mind on. I'm also deeply grateful to him for allowing me to share personal details of his story in this book, which helped me tell my own story more fully.

Whether we admit it or not, we need those people in our corner. People who work with us and share our impossible dreams.

It is never done alone.

Thank you all.

ABOUT THE AUTHOR

Saya Sakakibara grew up in a highly competitive environment alongside her brother, Kai, both of whom became professional BMX racers. Saya's love for BMX racing blossomed at just four years old, attending practice sessions and races with Kai. Over her twenty years in the sport, Saya has amassed an impressive collection of titles, including an Olympic gold medal. She credits her success to the support and challenges from her family – especially her father, brother and coaches – who pushed her to reach her full potential and develop her own drive and motivation.

www.ingramcontent.com/pod-product-compliance
Lightning Source LLC
Chambersburg PA
CBHW020516080526
44583CB00013B/616